JOURNEY THROUGH LIFE'S FLOW

A Memoir of Endurance and Hope

Christine Pimental

Copyright © 2024
All Rights Reserved

No part of this book may be reproduced or transmitted in any form or by any means, electronic or mechanical, including photocopying, recording, or by any information storage and retrieval system without the written permission of the author, except where permitted by law.

I dedicate my memoir first and foremost to GOD, the Most High, the Almighty, the Omega, my Creator. Secondly, I'm dedicating this book to my parents, Christine and Richard, for without them, there'd be no ME. I also dedicate this to my two siblings, Alicia and Lil Richie, whom I miss daily, but I know they're beside me, helping to guide me every step of the way in my life. My Nana, who I pray to amongst God, my parents, and siblings for guidance and strength every day. My three amazing children. Thank you for always believing in your mommy and never giving up on me, especially at times when I wanted to give up on myself. Thank you for being the amazing spirits that you are, loving me and showing me love that I never knew existed. To my nephew and two nieces, I love you and thank you for loving me. Just know that, just like my three children, you guys mean the world to me. I told your mom when she passed that I would never leave you guys, and I mean that. You three are not only my sisters' babies, but you're my babies, too.

I dedicate this book to everyone and anyone out there who has ever felt like they didn't belong. Like they are misunderstood or different. Who has ever been through things that made them feel like they were hard to love or broken? Like so much stuff has happened in their life to keep moving, keep going. Never give up. Learn to block out all the noise and distractions and LOVE yourself. Seek God, and he will always help and guide you through EVERYTHING and ANYTHING you may face. Understand and know that there's nothing you can't get through. "WINNING" is the only option.

I love you,

Christine.

Table of Contents

Prologue i

Chapter One 1

Chapter Two 8

Chapter Three 14

    Part I 14

    Part II 19

    Part III 28

Chapter Four 32

    Part IV 39

    Part V 47

Chapter Five 51

Chapter Seven 72

Chapter Eight 90

Chapter Nine 113

Chapter Ten 123

Acknowledgments 129

About the Author 131

Prologue

A Stoic philosopher, Heraclitus, once said, *"A person never crosses the same river twice. For it is not the same person, nor the same river."*

In the quiet corners of my memory, where my pain intertwines with joy and a blooming spirit comforts an aching heart, lies my tale of journeying through life in a constant flow of worries for the future, ecstasies of the present, the anxiety of trusting, the strength of speaking my mind, and an experience of making through life that is everything but. Life began to teach me its lessons at an early age. I have always maintained my resolve. I believe that despite the hard-hitting, bitter truths of life, we can endure and keep our heads up. We can walk with our chins up and stand tall, even though life makes its best attempt to make us crumble to dust. But sometimes, life takes its time and hits you when you least expect it. Or if that doesn't work, it will put us in a tough place, mentally and physically, and just see how long we take before we fall and submit to life. Cynically speaking, it just wants to have fun. Optimistically, the human spirit is much tougher than life itself. It only needs to believe in itself. That, I think, is the beauty of being a human. It can not only withstand all sorts of adversities but can find a silver lining in bleak, dark clouds and build the foundation for a new life to flourish. Make no mistake; this is a godly trait. We need only believe.

Everyone I've ever heard, read, and seen has always said that none of us know what life has in store for us, but no one ever said anything about what life doesn't. I learned that the hard way.

I have forgotten much of my childhood (intentionally). I have few memories of my mother. The ones I have, I resented for a long time because of her absence, but I don't remember any of my father. My sister and I have remained each other's only true family since I can remember. One of my almost forgotten memories is my parents naming me Christina Maria Allen. Born the youngest of three children to Christine and Richard, it has been a rollercoaster of emotions to dwell in resentment toward my parents for the use of drugs and, consequently, for abandoning my sister and me. Familiarity with 'home' had remained a mere concept for a long time.

Consistently being abandoned and taken up and abandoned again brewed abandonment issues that have taken all life to shake off. Seeing life being taken away to giving birth, I've never understood if memories fade to make space for newer experiences or better experiences replace the unfond ones. The struggle to understand the dichotomy of life is real. An even bigger mystery is how two people can perceive the same so differently that they end up walking absolutely opposite paths in life. I never accepted my sister's way of living. Maybe, I didn't understand her. Maybe, I was so caught up in my own storm that I couldn't see hers. Regardless. That's my blood. I pray for only the best for her.

From trying to understand what relationships should be like to making peace with the fact that it is our own fire that we need to kindle before we can go ahead to shine light upon others, one realizes and understands the famous quote the circles the in philosophy infused algorithms on social media applications and websites, "Hard times make strong people, strong people make soft times. Soft times make weak people. Weak people make hard times. Hard times make strong people and back again." The darkness of life can be and will only be kept at bay if we fan the flames within us and the ones we adore and love.

Without further ado, allow me to tell you how Christine saw the world and how the world has changed the way Christine sees it. This is my story, a memoir, my testimony of due diligence to find my small measure of peace in life.

Chapter One

May 22nd, 1985. That is the date I made my way into this world. I opened my eyes to see Christine, my mother. Even though I don't remember, maybe that is the fondest memory of my mother. Her addiction had taken her for a long time, even before I was born. My 'father', Richard, was a man who I have only unanswered questions about. I do know what he looked like, though not having met him, I feel as if he's only a fictional character in my life.

My knowledge of my biological father has been filled by my aunt, who adopted me after coming back to Massachusetts, and she didn't fill me in on any of the good stuff about him. Maybe there wasn't any about him, at least to her, there wasn't. All I was told was that they (Mom and Dad) moved in with their children into my aunt's house—Mom's biological sister's, when I was an infant. Perhaps, that's when my half-aunt developed her ill opinion of my father. Perhaps, she had it even before that. Maybe she doesn't know about Denver, Colorado. Neither do I, but all I know is that people from the Department of Social Services came to get me and my siblings when we got there. I was only three or four months old and sick when it happened.

Journey Through Life's Flow

I'm glad I can't remember much about it because when, for some reason, my parents decided to take my sister and me to Denver, Colorado, we were intercepted (*literally*) by the Department of Social Services. They separated us from our parents (for obvious reasons) and brought us back to Charlestown. The only place the child in me can call home. It is a lovely concept, isn't it? That of 'home'. A place where one can be free of all that is bad in the world, a safe haven. It is everything but walls, doors, and window panes.

I've always maintained that it is an enclosed space where multiple live together, and it is precisely those people who live there together who make it a home. When I moved into my aunt's, it was just one man who gave me that feeling of a home. Maybe, living with Mom and then with my aunt, ironically, taught me what a home should not be like. As a child, it was always easy to have that feeling. That is by being exactly their opposite.

All that I had perceived of my elders birthed within me a rebel who despised, dejected, rejected, and went against most of what my elders taught me. That included everything my aunt told me about my father. Venomous words about a man I have never seen with a conscious mind, my aunt never let an opportunity pass by where she could bash my parents. Yeah, he left my mother and my siblings and I, but he is my father. I don't know what it was that made me wonder so much about him.

By God, children are the flowers of Eden. There's no malice in them. All a child can think about is being attended to. That's all they think of. And if they're not catered to, they will take the world on their heads. I found that absolutely adorable. I didn't take the world up on my head. I imploded because that's all I thought of.

Regardless of my aunt's intense slandering of my biological father, I often wondered about who he was, how did he look, did he love his children, and if he did, then why didn't he come back? It was my mind mindlessly wandering into the darker corners of my mental space. It was precisely this wandering off the trail that brought me to all these questions, but they seemed like questions that would never be answered. But that was all it was. A fantasy. My mother had tried her best to raise her three children. It had been my childhood fantasy to live life with both parents, with every one of my family present and healthy.

Even my sweet, sweet boy. My brother. Unfortunately, he tragically died when he was just a year old. I have to be honest. I wonder less and pray more for my brother than I do or did for Dad. He was an innocent soul. He didn't have to leave. Or maybe, God favored him by not letting him see the mess that our parents had brought us in. I'm glad for him. It was gloomy. Blinding darkness. He died an infant, right before I was born. So by law, he went straight to Heaven. Good for him. He deserves the best. I envied him when I was young.

I was born while my mother abused drugs. I will not name what she used to do or how often she did it out of respect for her stature as a 'mother', nor do I know exactly. After all, she is the one who, despite preferring drugs over her children, gave me not a brother I can hug and hold when I need to but a brother I can look at in the picture on my bedside wall and talk about anything and everything to whenever I hoped for it. It is always great to pray to God for and about a handsome and wonderful boy who would've become a beautiful soul had he lived. I resented my mother for most of my life. It wasn't one thing but a series of reasons.

I had to not just forgive them both, but I needed to move on too. As time went by and I grew older, I understood an important lesson about life, and the most important for a child to know as they transition into an adult is that our parents, just like us, are human. They make mistakes, too. Only the terrible ones, though. One such mistake, which now I believe was one of the most beautiful moments of falling in love. Something to be written about. But it won't be me. Not right now, at least.

Being born to a woman in her rampant addiction days was not an easy start, frankly speaking. She didn't take care of her children when she should've. She didn't spend her money to take care of her children. She could've tried to quit her addiction. Maybe, life would've been better had she been high on love for her daughters. Or is it just something written in books or watched in movies? Whatever it was, it messed me up. I needed to find a way out of this rabbit hole. I didn't know what she was consuming when I was in her womb. All I know is that there have been instances where I was taken to multiple check-ups to diagnose any health condition. There came a time when I was being tested for AIDS because Mom had it as well. All those surgeries and medical checkups. It went as far as doctors telling my aunt that I won't live for long. Even if I do, I will have loads of health issues and conditions. I have issues, yes, but not what those doctors thought. They should throw their degrees out the window because I showed them, didn't I? That's how I know that there's a warrior in me who has just been making it through for most of my life. I was just making it through as the youngest of my family for sure.

Our maternal family is white, and we didn't know anyone on our father's side, so me and my sister were the only mixed kids growing up in a predominantly white community. It was both precious and detested. I grew up in the Bunkerhill Projects in Charlestown, Massachusetts. Yes, I'm a 'TOWNIE!' I was born and raised in a lovely, close-knit neighborhood. Charlestown was fun, and personally, although it was a predominantly Irish town, I never felt different, nor did anyone ever make me feel different. That's home, and for me, it always will be. The memories and experiences of growing up there have shaped and molded me to be the strong woman I am today. The strong, never back-down, tight, family-oriented ways of growing up there and seeing how everyone stuck together helps me to this day, even when it comes to raising my own children. Always having each other's back and always protecting each other. That's also what a family should do. But as fate would have it, I would not experience this at my aunt's.

The only true family I was able to spend quality time with was my sister, Alicia. She was the first child, as my mother would usually call her, lovingly but empty in entirety. She was my everything: my blood, friend, confidant, mentor, nemesis—EVERYTHING. No doubt, we had our fair share of fights, as siblings do.

Because of my resentment toward Mom, I preferred to stay with my aunt, when I could've visited Mom. Alicia, however, being the eldest, did spend time with her. She was much closer to her than I was. We didn't agree on the matter. We never did. I never understood why she would stay with her despite whatever our mother did.

My aunt was not a good person. Straight up. Her recurring racist remarks about anything that she sees about people of color made me question a lot of things about my own identity. She would, however, tell me that she is not talking about me and that I am better than them, but it's hard to shake off knowing that I, too, have some

Christine Pimental

Black in me. My mind would wander all over the place and wonder about her intentions. "Is she cussing at me? Am I the bad one? Or am I better because she said so?" All this mindless wandering brought me nothing but anxiety and more questions regarding my own ethnic identity. Seeing this, the man I gladly call Dad grew sympathy for me.

Chapter Two

Even though I'm not fond of the life my parents provided for me and my siblings, to say the least, the story of their time together is important to know for you so you may know why my life came to be the way it did. This is a difficult tale for me to tell, so bear with me.

As mentioned before, my mom's name is Christine, and my biological father's name is Richie. Despite their age disparity, Christine and Richie fell madly in love with each other. They both met at the notorious Combat Zone, where they both used to work. Yes, the notorious adult entertainment district that Mayor Raymond Flynn brought down in 1993. Today, one cannot believe strolling down the area of Chinatown on Washington Street between Boylston and Kneeland that, this used to be one of the most famous adult adult entertainment districts in all of Boston, Massachusetts. I understand if your curiosity runs wild, mine does as well but stop. They were my parents. Their work allowed them to meet each other frequently and build their relationship. Before they knew it, they were madly in love. Eventually, they decided to have children. So came into the world Alicia, my sister, Little Richie, my brother, and yours truly. Credit to them where it's due; they tried what they did to stand up on their feet and provide a living for their children. Unfortunately for them, and us as well, they could not.

Life went down the spiral rather quickly. My father went to prison on charges trumped-up against him before any of his children were born and stayed there until he was acquitted of all charges. After that, he continued to provide for his family along with my mother, but nothing came to fruition. After his acquittal and the birth of his children, things did not seem to run in their favor. For unforeseen circumstances, but in retrospect, regrettable ones, my parents and their children had to bounce around a lot. It got so bad that they had to move in with my aunt.

My mother tried harder but, much like my father, could not do much. She was put into jail when I was in my early childhood and stayed there up til I was in my early teenage. She was in the Massachusetts Correctional Institution in Framingham (MCI-Framingham). It is a medium-security prison for women in the South Middlesex Correctional Center. The whole time Mom was there, my anger and distaste for her grew slowly but consistently because of what my aunt was feeding into my ear regarding her behavior and her ability and potential to be a good mother. I only wanted to be taken care of by my own family. The child in me felt helpless. A father who had gone away, a mother who was imprisoned, and a sister, oh my poor sister, who was put in the path of the vile. I only desired one thing and one thing alone. To be welcomed and embraced into the arms of my own family. I do not understand to this day, nor can I fathom what God wanted from me, of me, to endure what I have endured. What did He want me to become? Maybe it is a question that will remain unanswered and perhaps an answer that I will take to my grave. Nana, my grandmother, would occasionally take me and my sister to go visit her in prison. I was always glad to see her face. To meet my mother was a blessing. One of the best and worst things that I could hope for. The best because I got to see how she was doing, and the worst because I got angrier every time I left after our meet-up. It was a weird feeling. Dad was locked up before my siblings, and I was born, and now my mother.

Mom did come back. When she got out of prison and came back, she was ecstatic. I mean, so was I. She would cook our cultural Filipino cuisines, and we would all have a good time. Finally, a part of my family who can sit and eat in peace. But not me. By that time, I had built up rage inside me. The whole time Mom was in prison, my wonderful aunt always filled my ears about how she abandoned us because she wanted to enjoy her own life, and since I was a naïve child, I believed my aunt. It made sense to an abandoned child and solidified my rage. I know I should not have believed her and should've put more faith in Mom. But it is exactly as they say, "Shoulda, woulda, coulda." Regardless of what I used to think, having Mom back was a wonderful feeling. If I ever needed to find her, I knew where I could find her. She was mostly found in the kitchen cooking Filipino food, and when she was not, she would be doing something else that would remind her of her Filipino roots.

I feel like she could notice that I had grown distant. She was a mother, and now that I am one, I know she knew what her children felt like. She tried her best for me to open up to her and talk to her about myself. She wanted me to let her in, but how could I? I had lost faith in the institution of 'family.' What was family anyway? How could a teenager know that nothing is thicker than blood? How could a child resolve her grievances on her own without anyone to talk to about it and forgive everyone, but mostly herself? How? I did not know how—at least for a long time. I did not let her into my world. She was not welcome at the time. No one was. Except one, which I will tell you about in a short while. It was one of the most difficult things I've had to do as a child. To let my own mother know what her child felt like. I cried tears of agony as I wrote the last sentence. No child should have to go through that ordeal. Not even my enemies and their children.

She eventually moved out of Nana's and got herself a program housing studio apartment. She would live there on her own for some time, and then later, Jimmy would come with her. Jimmy was her boyfriend, and he was amazing. Jimmy would take care of Alicia and me whenever we came over. He would make us feel like we were his own daughters. It was nice to have Jimmy around. I would occasionally spend nights over at Mom's apartment, and we would try to mingle and catch up about each other's lives. Alicia would sometimes join us as well. Those nights were like a slumber party. The three of us would eat together, watch TV together and sleep together. That is a beautiful memory. After all is said and done, isn't that what we are left with about the ones we love? The memories. The good and the bad. Both are cherished. That is a possession of mine that no one can take away.

Another beautiful memory from those days is Nana's dog that she gave to Mom. We would take Sandy on walks together and go food shopping and have a blast, really. That was another cherished memory, but here all credit goes to Sandy. It didn't have a worry in the world; it was not hurt by anyone, nor did it understand the horrifying intricacies of life. That dog would run wherever it wanted to, bark at whatever it wanted to, wiggle its tail at whomever it wanted to, and play whatever it wanted to. Such a gleeful dog. And what a life, by God, what a life she lived. That dog, in retrospect, was an inspiration to me in so many ways. Maybe, that's how life is supposed to be lived. Hanging onto the past is a terrible way to sabotage the present. We can only make most of the time that we have by living it fully, in the present, in its entirety, without a single remorse for the actions we did or the acts of others that affected us, directly or indirectly, without reservations or wanting to hold others accountable for what they did to us. These are shackles that hold us to our past and won't let us go. The harder we try, the worse it restricts us. Life is meant to be lived in the present without having to worry about what has happened before that moment or what will happen after. Unfortunately for yours truly, I didn't learn this lesson until later in life, but I am so glad I did. Better late than never, right?

I just want my mom to know that through my healing and having a better understanding of life her, her life. I forgive her, I appreciate her bring me into this world, I love her and miss her a lot.

Chapter Three

Part I

This lesson was taught to me by my sister, Alicia. Well, she did not do it intentionally, of course, but I did learn it with her help. Pro tip: If you want to let someone know how much you love them or what they mean to you, DON'T THINK about letting them know. Don't think at all. Just let them know that just by being in their presence, everything around them lights up.

The words that remain unsaid are the words that haunt us the most. So many words I kept, so many things I did not say, so many hugs I did not embrace and so many smiles I could not catch. I deprived my sister of them all and created a guilt for myself that would bring me back to the past every so often. It is not a pretty sight. Not something I would recommend a friend, in fact, quite the contrary. My brother had died before I was born. Looking at his picture on my bedroom wall, I talk about everything to him. I visit his grave occasionally but not enough. It is an emotional undertaking which, to be honest, I still am not able to fully shoulder. Even so, with him, I don't have to accommodate any remorse for not having said anything I wanted to. But with Alicia it is a different story. With Alicia, I feel as if I should've been there for her. I should've been a better sister.

My sister and I did not have a chance to grow up together because of unforeseen and unfortunate circumstances. A lot of times, I would be with our aunt when my sister would be with our mother or her adopted parents. We both did so for our personal reasons and beliefs. I did it not because I was attached to my aunt more than I was to my mother and sister, but because I despised my mother. Every now and then, I used to catch myself blaming her for everything—for having been put through a horrible childhood, for having lost so much of innocence and youth, for having to do things that children should not even be expected to do, for the being put in the pit that is life, because she could not uphold her end of being a mother and restraining herself of her indulgences for her children. I blamed it all on her. Consequently, at times, I grew apart from my sister as well, because, later she dwarfs me in spirit, courage, endurance, and just is a mammoth of a human being.

Gradually, as we grew older, I don't remember who it was or how it happened, but we began to converse. Maybe, it was only natural, which is why I don't remember how it happened. What I reminisce on frequently, is how beautiful and truly remarkable it was to have experienced that. Despite my should've, would've, could'ves, I mostly thank God for having blessed me with having lived my life with my sister, albeit, briefly. The time spent with her was the most magical time I have lived till yet. My visiting her kindled the bond, which was supposed to—should've—existed and flourished between us two sisters from the start. This didn't happen until we were older.

During our stays together, I would ask and she would tell me about her childhood. She once told me how our aunt used to abuse and torment her. She also told me about other types of abuses she endured. She also told me how another relative of hers sexually abused her. She would recount all these things with me. She did not have anyone else; just like me. It burned my heart and my blood, having listened to her stories. My sister … what a brave girl! I was so proud of her. But I wanted to hurt everyone who hurt her, but I couldn't. I felt miserable because the hurt on Alicia's face was conspicuous. She did not deserve that—no one does, and she went through it all. Even though, it was obvious during her recounts that it is not something she likes to think about—*talking about things helps sometimes*—she did not break. My sister was strong; she did not break a single tear. As a matter of fact, it was me who was the weaker one. Here was my sister, not shedding a tear even after talking about her traumas, and I cried because I was getting homesick. I mean, what? That sweetheart would comfort me and console me, because I would either sleep or keep crying. The feeling of being safe has been a rather rare feeling for me. That transcends all physical comprehensions when one feels safe under the shade of a sage. Undoubtedly, she was one.

Life did not give her a good caretaker as a child. Our aunt did not deserve to have raised my sister. She deserved more. Here, our uncle was a better option for her. Our uncle and aunt had had enough one day. They filed for divorce. They went their own ways. My uncle remarried and moved with his new wife.

Alicia didn't show me how hurt she was. *Why couldn't I give my sister that solace?* She, unfortunately, found that comfort in drugs and alcohol, and got addicted to them. I often ask myself, *Could I have done something to not let her be consumed by it or to stop her somehow from taking those drugs or drinking?* I went to a few of her therapy sessions to discuss bettering our bond. We were fighting ... frequently. I was scared that I would lose her, or she would leave me. Just as our parents did. The therapist told me not to let my past dictate what my present and future should entail. She said the same for her. I was to stop judging my sister and she was to stop judging me. We agreed. But we had a bone of contention that couldn't be resolved even with the help of a therapist. Mom. Whenever her name would come about in our conversations with each other, she would praise and defend her; I would disagree and always bring up how she left us. Those were more of the unpleasant sides of our relationship. She had grown extremely attached to her over the time she had spent with her. I, on the other hand, didn't. The only resolution we could find for the said disagreement was to agree to disagree. And we left it that. I loved my sister too much to give up on her. I will pull through. I will be there for her. So, we went on. I have felt as if she is my other half.

After Mom passed away, we got closer than we had ever been. I realized so much about me and Alicia that SHE AND I ARE THE SAME! We looked alike, sounded alike, and acted alike. Even what we would get triggered by and how we would act upon our anger was like each other's. We would tell each other everything and anything. How our day went, what we're thinking, whom we are dating, all of it. She was one of the first ones whom I told that I was pregnant and was going to have a daughter. My eldest daughter is THE blessing for me. Even before she was born, she had already gifted us one of the best gifts to me and my sister. She solidified our bond with each other. As soon as I broke the news to Alicia, we instantly, without even speaking a word to each other, knew that we were all we had left, and we needed to be together for the child I was about to bring into the world. Life was about to take a turn for the better now. In that moment, I was so excited for the future that was coming our way.

Part II

On the day I left my doctor's with my first daughter, Alicia was the first person we had seen, so we pulled over to show my daughter to her. Just seeing her broke me. She was not in a good place. She was out on the street, consuming the drugs she had turned to during her times of distress. I realize now that it's not drugs that are bad. I mean, they are, but the real evil is all the bad ideas and opinions that have formed inside the mind of the person who is consuming them. It is absolutely tragic that the most beautiful and loving souls feel so alone and unhappy that they are able to see nothing good in life. Consequently, they begin to take comfort in anything that helps them escape their reality. Alicia fell prey to this infinite, mindless, and pain-stricken tragedy. It was devastating to see my sister like this. I would've done anything and everything to pull my sister out of this pit. All I did was fight and blame her for the choices she was making. Maybe things would've turned out differently had I changed my approach to her. I genuinely thought that the child that came into our lives would make her come out of it on her own.

On my way back home, that's when I saw her. Even though I didn't want to introduce my daughter's aunt to her in the state Alicia was in, I could not deny her that happiness, knowing what she had gone through all her life. I will never be able to forget the way her face lit up when she saw her niece for the first time. Who can imagine the happiness that such a tiny person can bring to someone? She could. Maybe she could not say what she actually felt, but her eyes and her face said everything they could. All I remember her telling me is, "She is so beautiful, Christine. She has her mother's eyes." Whenever I reminisce on this moment, tears fill my eyes. Becoming a mother for the first time, Alicia becoming an aunt, and my baby rejoicing with both her women. By far, it was one of the most beautiful moments of my life, and that too, with my whole family at the time. I will cherish it always. Because soon, Alicia and I were not going to be on speaking terms.

A few years later, Alicia gave me the best pre-birthday gift ever. She was pregnant with her firstborn. She brought her son into the world just a day before my birthday. My family was getting bigger, and Alicia and I were over the moon. We were both mothers now. It was the most beautiful time of my life to date. And it was about to get even more beautiful. Our firstborns had an amazing bond between them, and it is impenetrable. Just a month before Alicia brought her son into the world, my doctor told me that I was pregnant again, and this time, IT WAS A BOY!! We both were mothers and now, we were both going to have boys. It has been the most amazing feeling being a mother. It is laborious, no doubt, but it is extremely rewarding. Even more so when you have a sister who is a mother herself.

Christine Pimental

I remember that in my initial days of potty-training my son, I faced extreme difficulty getting him to hit the target. Although I love my boy, his inability to do so was becoming a nuisance. I felt as if this boy was never going to learn, and he would be embarrassing himself in the years to come. She asked if she could keep him over the weekend, particularly to train him and to paly with my nephews. I had already tried everything I could to make it work but to no avail. So I let her keep him briefly. To my surprise, when my son came home after a weekend with his aunt, he was a professional! I don't know what she did, said, or conditioned him to do, but it worked like a charm. I asked her, later on, what she did to make him understand.

She told me, "I put a Cheerio in the toilet bowl and asked him to aim at it."

When she told me this, all I could do was laugh. This had become so much of a pain for me that I couldn't handle it, and she fixed it for me in just one weekend. To this day, I am indebted to her for all that she did for me, but most importantly, for being an amazing sister, an even better aunt, and for just being an overall incredible human being.

As time passed, she broke the news to me that she was pregnant with her second child, my niece. Little did she know that three months before she gave birth to my niece, I was pregnant with her youngest niece. We both were about to have girls together. Both our daughters are sisters from other misters, but their bond is even thicker than blood.

A few years later, on St. Patrick's Day, she gave birth to my youngest niece. I would often tease Alicia about it because she never liked to claim our Irish side.

One thing my sister and I bonded over a lot was our relationships. The relationships we used to be in were quite different, but the issues we faced while we were in them were quite alike. So, when we used to argue and quarrel with our boyfriends, we would bounce off each other what we were going through, what ideals were, how we would like our problems resolved, what would be a realistic approach to the problems we faced, etc. It wasn't usually the best of scenarios for our boyfriends, but for us as sisters, it was everything. Finally, I had a family who was there for me when I needed them, helping me out when I was troubled, contributing to my family, and helping each other out. Isn't that what family is all about? Just being there for one another.

At the beginning of our teenage years, Alicia and I had a fight over a situation that transpired between us. I held and resented her as I believed she inflicted what she did on purpose. Years later, she told me her side, and all was resolved. But the damage to our bond and trust had been done by then. This was one of the major causes of our on-and-off relationship. We both grew out of it. She certainly did, but I can't say the same for myself, even though I thought I was. That may or may not have played a part in our escalated quarrel years later, which was to be our last fallout.

One night, she called on my cell phone. She was messed up: high, drunk, and intoxicated with God knows what. What struck a nerve for me was that my oldest, my daughter, and my firstborn picked up the call. She asked her something along the lines of if my daughter thinks her biological dad cares or loves her. My daughter's father and I had made a consensual decision of not being together, so I decided to raise her on my own. We were both young and in love, but too young and immature to put our child first. I had kept that a secret from my daughter to the best of my abilities. She did not need to know anything about it, as I had lived with the pain of an absent biological father all my life. I was prepared to let her know one day. That, too, was to be influenced by a lot of cushions and fabrications in order for my daughter to take it in without breaking. I would often think about how to do it, too. Never had I imagined that this idea would be seeded in my daughter's mind by my sister, her aunt. I was infuriated. However, the real reason why I felt my blood boiling was much more petty than that.

By this time, Alicia had lost her children due to her addictions, and this reminded me of our own parents and how our mother lost us before losing herself, even though she desperately wanted to be with her children. My rage took the best of me.

I confronted her on the matter. I was hurt and felt betrayed. I was all over the place. We argued. So much.

In a heated conversation such as this, with the emotional stake that it carries, I will always recommend keeping a mediator between the two people or parties. God knows I needed one that day. In retrospect, I, perhaps, should've taken her to therapy or even as much as have kept a mediator there to help control the overflow of emotions, which were sure to be spilled.

The argument went on to the point that I was ready to strike her. I didn't do that. So, I did the next worst thing. I lashed out at her. I said so many things and was so out of line. I didn't care at the moment that she was my sister, my only family, or even that she was a human who could feel. The next worst thing was actually THE WORST thing to do. I should've just struck her. Had I hit her, I would've saved our bond, but I chose not to. I was relentless. The hurt showed on her face; her eyes began to squint, and her lips quivered, but I didn't stop. I had tasted the corruption of bludgeoning someone's heart. I was consumed by it. All this time, I had judged her for being intoxicated by drugs, yet here I stood, intoxicated, corrupted, and completely consumed by the high of hurting someone I love so much so that I could feel better. I could not have been more wrong. This regret I will remorsefully take to my grave. By my own admission of the crime I committed, I have yet to stand in front of

Alicia and beg for forgiveness and apologize for not caring for the only family I had after my children.

She tried to reach me through my boyfriend at the time to patch things up. She would regularly tell my boyfriend in the day to tell me that she loved me and missed me. My stubborn brain did not want to fix it. I was raging. She tried everything to reach out to me, and I would always shun her. Little did I know that, later in life, this was to become my deepest regret.

We would often glance at each other in passing during football matches where our sons and my eldest daughter played and cheered for Charlestown, Massachusetts. Our hometown. During one of the game and cheerleading practices, I walked on the ramp to the field, and she was coming up toward me. We both passed by each other as if we didn't even know each other. We didn't tilt our necks; we didn't stop to say hi; we refused to recognize each other. This was to be the last time that I was to ever see her. I should have stopped. I should've held her arm and forced her to stop. I should've called out her name. I should've told her that I am not ready to live without her. I should've … I …

A few weeks later, my adopted mother called me and broke the news to me. I couldn't believe my ears. I immediately dialed my sister-mom (my uncle's wife.) She kept repeating, "I'm sorry. I am so sorry." Alicia was no more. She had gone to a better place. Leaving me with the guilt of a lifetime. The weight of the sorrow, the guilt, the remorse, the pain of letting multiple opportunities pass by to make it up with her. I was broken. I felt as if I had lost everything. I felt as if there was nothing more to live for.

On the way to her funeral, while in the car with my three children and their dad, I looked over to him while he was driving and said, I'm never going to be the same after this."

He looked at me and said, "I know."

Everything in my life changed after that day, my perception, my opinions…everything about myself. The most that had bothered me and messed with my mind at that point was that now I knew. Me and Alicia were the last children of my parents, and with her demise, it meant that I was all alone in the world now. Yes, I did have my children and my boyfriend with me, but all my relatives, all my family, all of my blood, was gone. My fear of abandonment escalated into overdrive. My mind raced with thoughts that were all over the place. I had lost all sense of purpose, all meaning in life; I was utterly distraught and had no one to lean on to be comforted. Not that I didn't have people who I loved more than life itself, it was just that I had lost all hope in life. I was suicidal.

I somehow managed to walk inside the funeral home, which, in that moment, seemed like the most difficult thing I've had to do in life. Reality hit me when I saw her laying in the casket. SHE WAS REALLY GONE! I couldn't face it…I couldn't face her…I could not deal with the pain. My inability to face what I was seeing before my eyes made me want to turn around and leave, but I knew I must see Alicia. I needed to fix her hair one more time…I needed to caress her cheek after all this time…I needed to speak to her one last time. I promised her, before I left the funeral, that I would never leave her children's side, and I won't! That was my promise to her. I will never leave her children's side, and will stand with them, no matter what.

Part III

The weight of that day trampled me into a crumble that I could not reel from for the most time. Walking out of the funeral home, a burning sensation in my heart kept reminding me that a huge piece of me had died with her, and I would never be able to fill that void. My boyfriend had held my arm throughout the funeral. Had I not had him that day with me, I do not know if I would have been able to stand that day, let alone walk in and out of the funeral home. I was filled with the vilest of thoughts, the most remorseful of emotions, and so much to cripple my belief that I had done good or even satisfactory in life. All this time that I had spent with her, I had not realized that, despite our fights, quarrels, arguments, and disagreements, she was the one who was keeping me alive. She was the one in whom my heart dwelled. She was the only one whom I kept thinking about. And now that she was gone, I felt my soul leave my body. I cannot describe that any better than saying that I was as if someone was pulling a silk cloth off of thorn bushes, and I was the silk cloth.

After the funeral and going through the most traumatic instance that I've had to endure in life, I could not live the way I used to. I did not think from a healthy mindset, to say the least. I didn't want to go out; I didn't want to do anything; I didn't plan anything to do; I could not even face Alicia's children. I had lost all willpower to pursue life. I know of depression, as in I understand what it means and what is the theory of it. But I do not know what it feels like to be in crippling depression. Yet, here I stood at a moment in time where I could not conjure the minutest drop of a little hope. Here, I tasted the flavor of being completely lost in life. My sleeping patterns were derailed off of the normal sleeping schedule. I was not eating what I should have and when I should have been. I was unable to think properly, make decisions, do my chores, take care of my kids, spend time with my boyfriend, tend the house: nothing. Seeing everything Alicia and I had built up all this time, individually and collectively, was crumbling down right before my eyes, and that was just adding to the fire. The scorching fire that had set ablaze all my rationality. My rashness was drifting all my loved ones away from me. My boyfriend, my mom who had adopted me, my own kids, and Alicia's more so. If I was not able to handle the loss of my sister, what did the kids who lost their mother feel like? I could not come to terms with the answer to that question. I was unable to take it. I could not handle it. Every time I looked at her kids, they reminded me of her. They have her eyes and her spirit in them. Whenever they stood before me and after I had spent time with them, I would cry till my eyes would feel so heavy that I couldn't open them up properly. I had no power in me to keep living. I was on the brink of committing suicide.

I took some time off from meeting them and took time out for myself. They were a constant reminder of her. I didn't know what to do at this time in my life. I had built an insanely negative perception of life, and my brain was conjuring up all the toxicity from anywhere and everywhere it could. I had to re-evaluate where I was standing in life. But then, something struck a thought in me. My promise to Alicia.

In my time away from them, I tried to improve everything I found to be ruined during my time of grief. Then came a time when I was only missing my nephews and nieces. I was always wondering what they were doing; *had they eaten anything? Were they sleeping alright? Are they missing their mom a lot? What kinda question is that? Of course, they are. They need someone to be there for them.* And that was it. I realized that not only was I being cruel to them by not being there for them, but I was doing myself a great injustice. They were the last gift of Alicia to me. They were the last memory I have of her…of my family.

I kept thinking about them in the days to come, that too throughout the day. I missed them so much that I went back to them. I went back with an evolved perception. A much better perception and improved health, both mentally and physically. I did not see it as a loss anymore. It was, no doubt. However, the gain which I had failed to see for so long was so much more than what I had lost. Now, I could see that I always had a piece of her with me. All I needed to make sure was that they always had a piece of her in me as well. My goal was determined. I had my own three kids, who are my biological children, but then I had six. The three of Alicia's who were precious to me more than life itself. After all, they were the ones who made me believe in life again.

I had found the missing pieces of my life. They were exactly six. Three I already had with me, but it was like I was missing half the puzzle. My other three children made me whole again. There was no doubt that I had lost all of my senses and then regained them back just by being with my six adorable, beautiful, incredible, and divine children. From then on, everything I have done in life has not been without deep consideration for them. I have made every possible decision to further improve my own jobs and way of living, but all that has been done to provide my kids with only the best of both worlds. I had decided that I was going to fulfill my promise to Alicia. Now, I was not just going to live for myself. My greater goal in life had become to protect my six children. All my decisions, actions, thoughts, and energy were going to be for them. Life was about to get better again.

Chapter Four

Other Siblings

As I mentioned earlier, childhood was a difficult phase for me growing up. I have elaborated on it in much detail in the preceding chapters. However, an important detail I did not reveal yet is that when I moved in with my aunt, she already had two children of her own, and both of them were older than me.

Yes… I began losing my sense of optimism quite early on. I never understood what they actually thought of me. Did they consider me to be their sibling the way I thought of them? Did they feel comfortable around me to joke around so freely with me? Were they genuinely themselves when they would try to prank me into something that would harm me, or did they intend it? I could've never truly understood that.

It began to bother me a little too much to sweep it under the rug. So, I had to come up with a label to put on it for my own sake, and I settled for jealousy. That was the only thing that made sense to me. Like all siblings, we had our fair share of quarrels but would make up about it instantly. There were both good times and bad times in my interactions with my "siblings", but I try to reminisce only on the good times. Had it not been the matter of writing this book, their memory might've been lost somewhere in my subconscious. I began suppressing their memory as by thinking of them, I would often always stray onto the not-so-enduring memories.

I mostly find myself going back to one particular memory. I don't remember exactly what age I was then, but most definitely under the age of 10. And my aunt's two eldest were alone in a room, and the eldest switched off the lamp in front of us. One of them asked me to kiss the switched-off lamp. I, being the young and naïve kid I was, obliged. As soon as my lips touched the bulb, my lips began to feel as if they had been smeared by molten lava. They began to burn instantly! I jolted off of the bulb and immediately started rubbing my lips to put out the burning sensation on them but to no avail. All the while I was trying to make myself feel better, I saw my "siblings" laughing erratically, with their backs hunched, and both of them high-fiving each other as if to commemorate each other for executing an excellent prank. And there I was, hurt, embarrassed, disgusted, and shocked. All at the same time. But that was not the last of it that I had gone through.

Another time, the same two elders of the household were playing with me on the first floor of my aunt's house. I do not exactly remember what we were playing or how events transpired, but what I distinctively remember is that each of them had one of my legs in their grip, and I was dangling upside down from the window of our house in the projects. I kept screaming for help, but they wouldn't pull me up. Instead, they chose to mock me and taunt me before letting both my feet go. I came crashing down on the ground. I later became immensely grateful to have unconsciously turned my body mid-air. Had I landed on my head, as per the logic of the fall, I might not have been alive to tell or even live the tales I am recounting in this book. It was reasons like these that solidified my opinion that I did not belong there... with them.

It became quite difficult for me to be able to cope with what had transpired in my life and then with what I was dealing with my "siblings". I was in a constant state of, at least, identifying why they were behaving the way they were. I still haven't made up my mind. But, as I said earlier, they had developed ill feelings towards me because they had presumed that I was going to take their mother away from them. My aunt did give me a lot of attention and attended to me whenever I needed anything. This had perhaps brought about in them this jealousy. I had felt that my aunt only catered to me because I was younger than them and also because of what I had gone through so early in my life. Since I had been deprived of motherly love myself, I was never able to relate to it. But now that I have become a mother myself, I see what needs a child has. I have based my motherhood, as normally mothers do, on a trial and error basis, but my experiences of life up till the present enable me to make my decisions keeping in mind all the parties involved in the decision, especially my six children.

It did not make complete sense to me in those days, but I realized I was poking a nerve that they are not liking. I began to ask for care less and less from my aunt. I believed if they saw less of me being taken care of, they would stop believing that I was the favored one. Their ill feelings, even though temporarily, subsided. I began to live freely and started doing things on my own. One of my favorite memories from this time of my life was riding my purple and pink big-wheel tricycle. One time, me and the second to eldest were riding my tricycle and were out and about. Suddenly, we started going really fast. So fast that the big wheel skidded on the ground, and we both fell. I tumbled with the tricycle and got myself a scraped knee in the process. It hurt a lot when I saw it, and I even have the scar from that accident to this day. But I had fun that day, so I didn't make much of the wound. So it was good and bad both with my siblings, but we only reminisce with a smile, or we don't at all.

During my teen, and especially during my preteens, I would mostly hang out with my second to eldest sibling. She lived with our dad (adopted dad, but my real dad in my eyes), and anytime I was to stay with Dad, we'd hang out. Growing up, she was probably my first-ever friend. We would stay inside the house and talk about anything, really. Sometimes, her friends would come over, and we all would go hang outside. And when they didn't and not even she was ready to hang out, I would go outside by myself and play or do anything I wanted on my own. He treated me like his own and always called me his daughter. He was the only person in my childhood with whom I found security, safety, and compassion. He was the knight in shining armor of my life. So, with his blessings, I could and did whatever I wanted.

This made my life with my siblings much easier, and we went to have some really good times, which have now become a great memory for me. Another great memory I have with my siblings is going to the "Hard Knock Life" concert in 1999 by Jay-Z, and even DMX (RIP) made the stage there. The ensemble consisted of big names in hip-hop like Methodman, Redman, and the Ruff Ryders. The icing on the cake was that we were in the second row, on the floor seats. The artists seemed super close to us. It was surreal! It was one of the best nights of my life. Me and my siblings, despite our differences, were also able to create fond memories for ourselves. I hope they reminisce about the good times of the past as I do.

Living with Dad was awesome. He would take care of me and all of his family. He was a true father figure that my life had so dearly missed. But sometimes, when he was not around, I would hang out with, my biological aunt, and my two younger siblings. They were fun to be around. I missed my sister in those days and especially the feeling of being a sister. These two babies made me feel like the elder sister I wanted to be. I liked spending time with them. They recognized me as their older sister, and I knew I could be true and honest with them.

They would come to me often with questions they did not feel comfortable asking their mother. I never understood why they did not go to our elder siblings, nor did I ever ask. Besides, I enjoyed our bonding time together. They mostly had questions about their bodies. I didn't tell them anything otherworldly, only what I knew. I told the girls that our bodies change and grow with age and that it is completely normal. There is probably a point in every girl's life where she is concerned to the point of a nervous breakdown of her own body. It is precisely during these times when young girls need their elder sisters, mothers, or, if not them, any woman of age who can help them understand their bodies. We would talk about puberty and female hormones, among other things. These were wonderful bonding moments between the three sisters.

It was especially of immense value to me because after my own home was wrecked, I had searched for a place to belong. Perhaps it was the sense of belonging I missed that might've made me feel at home anywhere I got it from. I like to believe it was God's way of watching out for me to allow me to have one of my most desired feelings from my two little sisters. Talking to them, educating them, and sharing moments with them made me feel a sense of belonging with them that I had missed for the most time in my life up till then. It was one of the most humbling moments of my life and one that I am extremely grateful for. Just the thought that they believed they could confide with me brought me enormous pleasure. It was the first time I had truly lived life in its truest sense. I happen to believe that life is best lived when it is shared with people you love. And it becomes even better when those closest to you trust you, and the best is when they feel safe with you. My two younger sisters were a blessing in my childhood, whom I will always remain grateful. Unlike most of the good things in my life, they still are in contact with me and reach out to me whenever they have questions they want answered or would just like to talk from time to time. They are one of the few people who have made me want to become a better person and pursue a better life.

Part IV

Other times, when I'd be at home, I'd hang out with my oldest sibling. We would watch sports or whatever we found appealing on T.V. But, mostly sports, and, especially, football. Initially, I did not even know what I was watching, but for jacked-up guys squashing each other trying to get a ball over to the other team's side—yeah, that didn't make much sense to me either. I felt my interest in football was close to naught. I was only obliged to watch it because it felt like a great bonding activity. She and I would laugh, cheer, scream, jump, and whatnot. Mostly her, but I rallied behind her, too. She eventually had to teach me some of the rules like, why are the guys smashing their shoulders against each other? Why are they running to the opposite side of the field? Why are they kicking the ball between the giant tongs? She explained it all, and suddenly, it all started to make sense. I also began to enjoy it even more. So now, we both laughed, cheered, screamed, and jumped equally. It wasn't all rainbows and butterflies with her as well.

More often than I can count, we both had what I call sibling conflict. I believe, as a younger sibling, you inherently consider your elder sibling as the epitome of coolness, calm, and tranquility. My elder sibling definitely had the charisma, and I looked up to her. So, as you can guess, I did venture off into her wardrobe. I did try her clothes and perfumes. As soon as I did, I felt a surge in my confidence. Maybe her clothes were made out of magic. Well…she didn't think so. Particularly because I was wearing them, she didn't stand that one bit. So many times, we argued over the said matter. She would scream, yell, cuss at me, and ridicule me. She would say so many things.

This is a good time to explain something to you guys about me. I do not align my boundaries properly with anyone, especially with people I adore. In fact, I blur my boundaries intentionally if I like you enough. But then comes the point, as I have often felt through my experiences when people try to intimidate you to get their way. As I find it, the purpose of the unnecessary audible screaming is to frighten the other(s). It has a weird way of altering the thought patterns of the brain instantaneously. That just works for me the wrong way. I have never been able to understand why it does me what it does. All I know is that it flips my fight-or-flight response to annihilate. And so it was inevitable whenever my elder would scream at me with her over-the-top reactions, I would reciprocate and throw a few punches of my own.

It generally remained arguments and heated verbal exchanges. However, there were times when water would get over the bridge. Then, the verbal jabs would turn into literal punches, scratches, and hair pulls. It was chaos…it was mayhem, and we were the ones who brought the havoc to our home. The regularity of our quarrels soon caught the eyes of our mom. It was more so the loud screeches and screams that actually annoyed her. The poor woman would be cooking us food in the kitchen, and suddenly, daunting yells from hell would rip through the house. The tranquil sanctity of the household would be transformed into a riotous pit. She had to intervene.

Unfortunately for me, I would always be blamed for the fights. The premise under which that judgment was passed was that I was the younger and, more importantly, the fighter. Now I did not agree that I would always be at fault just because I am the younger one. But, I had no case against the latter allegation. I had to plead guilty. I did so often that it staled my relationship with my sibling. It became unpredictable. I had to be on my toes every time. For me, if I am with a beloved, I'd rather put all my guard down, be absolutely free of fears of judgment, and be in serenity as I have conversations with them. Perhaps, we did have that at some point in life, but over the years, due to our regular fighting and one-sided resolutions, our bond was slivered.

As I have already elaborated, I'm not much of a talker. I find it a ginormous task to express myself. I'm more often stuck between "Have I completely said what I wanted to?" and "What is the way I can express the most?" And almost always, I would end up saying nothing at all. Everything would be suppressed inside. I used to hold many grudges with people I couldn't speak to freely without realizing it was my responsibility to let them know in the first place before expecting anything back. You guessed it right—I am an overtly over-thinker. It has mostly been a curse, but it has been a great blessing as well, but, we'll get to that later.

The one thing that my two elder siblings repeatedly threw at my face whenever we would be in the arguments in question was Mom. The fact that she wasn't around. The fact that Dad was nowhere to be seen. The fact that my whole family was derailed. They didn't, perhaps couldn't, empathize with an experience completely alien to them. They lived in their own house, with their own parents, with their own siblings. Maybe they did not know at all of the trauma it wreaks. I do understand that, and I can empathize with where they were coming from. What I could not empathize with was why they intended to cut so deep. They frequented their mocking with laughter and ridicule. Knowing me, it is needless to say that our whole relationship turned toxic and abusive. Soon, it became a lost cause. It was different with my younger siblings. Look…I know that siblings have their fair share of conflicts, but that is all that they are—arguments and conflicts. The moment they trespass over to slivering and cutting deep, it tarnishes the sanctity of even a familial bond. It is so, at least in my opinion.

I realized beyond doubt how flip-floppy my relationship with my older siblings had become later on in my young adult life. After I had my firstborn, I moved in with my oldest sibling. Her father would come in from morning to nighttime to help out in raising our daughter.

Christine Pimental

It was a great moment for me to raise a family of my own, and that too, with all of them present. It was a big deal for me to have become a mother for the first time and to be raising my child alongside her father. The only problem for me was that the house I was raising my family in was not my own. My eldest sibling was irked by my eldest daughter's father coming into the house. I never got my head around as to why she was irritated by him. She even confronted me about it and told me to stop him from coming to the house and that I would have to take my child and leave if he did not stop. That right there was her vintage, over-the-top reactions. He was nothing but nice to her, and, most of all, he was a concerned father who was trying to be present for her child. That was more than what she had.

The fathers of her children were unfortunately not present for her children. One was in jail on trumped-up charges, so to speak, and the other…well, personally, I don't think she wanted him around anyway.

I still wanted my daughter's father to be present in her life, so I would sneak him into the house without my oldest sibling knowing about it. It was a little exciting. To be doing something I'm told not to. Is that messed up? Anyways. It was becoming a nuisance not just for me but also for him, and due to many other reasons as well, he eventually stopped stopping by. The whole scenario that had transpired sparked in me a resolution. A resolution that would prove to be a milestone for me and my daughter.

I moved into a shelter with my baby because it had dawned on me as the truth of all truths. I needed my own space to raise a family. This transcended the realm of opinion to reality when I accidentally found a letter she had written to her boyfriend in jail, in which she, in so many words, talked about how she was annoyed, irritated, and tired of me being there, and wanted me out of the house. It is important to be clear here that during my stay with her, I did not live there for free.

Because I was no longer working, she convinced me to apply for welfare benefits. It seemed to work for her, as now I do nothing but watch over my daughter. For her, it became a way to live her life the way she wanted by going out and dating again without worrying about the responsibility of looking after her children, which I didn't mind.

After I got myself a place in the shelter, I began to date again and would usually stay at her house on the weekends. I would call my boyfriend over and hang out with him, and that, TOO, was a bother for her. She asked for him to stop coming over as well. That was it! I stopped going over to her place from then on and spent my weekends with him until I got my own apartment.

Regardless of what my opinion of her is, one thing that she deserves credit for is being an awesome godmother to my daughter. She would buy her new shoes and clothes, all the stylish stuff, when my daughter was younger. She would take care of her as her own daughter. Evidently, she never acted toward my daughter, keeping my bias in her. I will always credit her for that.

But…hear me out on this one…she did cross the line with my boyfriend at the time. He is the father of my youngest two. I cannot believe, as I write this, that my eldest sibling accused him of a severe allegation that got him into a lot of trouble. What surprises me more is that she did that to me despite the fact that, prior to that, she was dating my boyfriend's friend, and they were even living with each other. Unbeknownst to her, her boyfriend in jail was released; perhaps he wanted to surprise her, but it was really him who got the surprise. Let's just say all hell broke loose when he found out about the guy living with her. We no longer speak, and I am least bothered by it.

Based on retrospect, she never meant any good to me. She did to my daughter, but then again, she was MY daughter. Life and memories with her had bothered me so much that I had to find a resolution for it. I forgave her. For all the times I spent with her that caused pain in my heart, I forgave her. I never agreed that she deserved the benefit of the doubt, but I had to forgive her for myself. I cannot keep such an ill feeling inside me for long. I feel as if I am being consumed by it. I forgave her so that I could move in life, and I did. It was a relief, a feeling of someone pulling weight off of my chest as if I could breathe again. It was unfortunate, perhaps, to have a tainted familial relationship, but I hope it has worked out for the better for both of us. I sincerely do.

Part V

Since I was not able to have such an ecstatic experience, I got more attached to my second-to-eldest sibling. I believe I have elaborated on my experiences with her in childhood. Later on in life, I got closer to her and became the one with whom I talked about more intimate things about me. But, after all the vile incidents that took place between me and her sister, I began a journey... a journey of realization and, more importantly, acceptance.

She partook in the infliction I felt for the longest time in my life, albeit not so much. Apart from helping her with her oldest child, I also helped to watch her firstborn, her son, while she worked. Despite knowing more about me, which made me believe that she would have more empathy, she did not appreciate it the way I expected her to. It solidified a long-reigning feeling inside me. A feeling of being unappreciated. Regardless of what I had done for the people whom I adored, I always felt that they couldn't feel it the way I felt. It built so much unease in me, to say the least, that I chose against what I had been doing my whole life... to be validated.

I distanced myself from everyone. I brought my communication with everyone I had previously spent my life with to a devastating halt. I stopped talking to my two 'elder siblings'. Even the younger siblings, who used to talk to me about everything, stopped talking to them as well. I did remain guilty for some time because of that, because I loved them like my own younger siblings, and they never did anything wrong to me, as a matter of fact, on the contrary. I did what I did for myself. I needed to go away… I needed to be at peace… I needed my own space.

This did not come about overnight or even in a fortnight. It came about due to many years of enduring subjugation from my relatives. All that one can expect to endure from people who despise you and hate you and want the worst for you; I felt that with my siblings and other relatives. Perhaps the reason why I would do so much to appease them was because I wanted to be validated by them, and that's where the journey began… should I be looking for validation from others, or should it be something I'm looking for inside my own self? I did not even have the slightest clue about it, even though I realized that I used to subconsciously look for it every day, in every interaction, every moment. This had to come to a stop, and I had no clue about how to go about it. For a long time in my life, I felt lost.

I began looking for the reason why I used to do so much to appease others. Immediately, I went back to my childhood. The traumas, the fights, the irrational screaming… need I say more? But having come so ahead in life, I had come to an epiphany. The love that I had showered on everyone was the love that I should've been giving to myself. This was the first realization I had come upon. The second was to develop the will and then the courage to say no to things you don't want to do or what you do not agree with just because you feel pressured into doing it. Third, detach yourself from places where you feel unappreciated or feel like you are becoming too toxic for your mental well-being. I found that it is important to take care of your own self and your mental state in an unforgiving world.

In the end, it was a difficult realization and an extremely rough lesson to learn, but maybe that's the thing. You have to learn these lessons on your own; otherwise, life will teach you, and life is one cruel teacher. Maybe loving from afar is not the worst thing. It does not necessarily have to mean that you dislike or even hate the person(s). It just means that you are in need of a space from which you can heal. Perhaps it is tough for some to realize that the solace they search for in others exists in themselves, and that too since birth. The logic behind it is that the person who knows you the most and the longest is your own self. One can lie to anyone; perhaps one can even manipulate everyone. But… one cannot lie to their own self. You know everything about yourself; there's nothing hidden about you from yourself. You know too much about yourself to keep it quiet. If you have deprived yourself of the mundane joys of life, if you've kept yourself away from the little glees, you are bound to go to war with yourself. Unfortunately, I had left myself stranded in the middle of nowhere in the context of taking care of myself, and I had had enough.

After all the distance that I had built between me and all the ones who I felt had wronged me, it was beginning to weigh on me. I had not yet made peace with my demons. I had to come to terms with the fact that I had to take the reins of my life into my own hands. I have my babies with me, and they have only their mother to take care of them. This made me take a stand. Perhaps it is right as they say, "You do not know how brave you are until being brave is the only choice you have."

I do not hold any grudge against anyone. I hold only myself accountable. After all, it was me who made all those decisions to be complicit in everything and anything that was asked of me. Maybe I was naïve to think that I would remain surrounded by all the people who have nothing but love for me. Well, I do… for everyone. I was so loving that I forgot to give myself any. This was about to change… completely.

Chapter Five

Dad

With consistent learning about the ways of life due to my constant experiences of belittlement and being dealt a card worse than the last in terms of circumstances in life, I finally was on my own. Completely… recklessly… naively… at my own discretion for well-being. But, surprise! Surprise! My knight in shining armor, my best friend, my savior, my dad.

As of April 5th 2023, my angel had done everything in him and beyond due to everything he took upon himself for raising someone else's child as his own. I'm all over the place talking about a man who has been everything in life for me. He protected and provided for me and much more. This man has contributed as a father, husband, son, friend, brother, and human, and was the one person God sent for me out of mercy, for whom I do not miss a chance to offer my gratitude. Let me tell you a story about a superhero who did not wear a cape.

In my younger years, he used to work for Boston Housing Authority as a truck driver. His job was extremely laborious as he would be transporting a lot of stuff and would be on the road for most of his day. Yet, he would take time out for his "angel", as he used to call me. He truly loved me like his own daughter. While I used to live with my aunt, he would come to pick me up in one of his trucks, and then we would go to have ice cream… and long drives… and have the time of my life. In retrospect, I should've asked for time to stop instead of ice cream at that point, and Dad would've done it. He never rejected any request from me, so much that the phrase, "If Duke cries, Daddy buys," won't be untrue. That was the nickname he used to call me. He parented me by letting me roam free and do the most childish acts that one can imagine from a kid… yes, that's it. He let me be a kid and trusted that I would find my own way. Even I did not have the belief he had in me. Sometimes, he would pick me up from Head Start Daycare; we would go have ice cream again! Or a slush this time. He never minded but, in fact, would let me take the lead and ask me what my plan was. Many a time, I would take my bike out and he would always be there every step of the way and every revolution of the wheel. He saw it all. From the scared little girl to the woman I have become, the departed soul has been by my side throughout.

On the weekdays, I would stay with my aunt, and on the weekends, holidays, vacations, or any other time when I would not have school, I would be with my dad. It was comforting to stay with him. There are so many memories, but the feeling I remember the most is not wanting to leave his side.

During the summers, we would drive up to my aunt and dad's sister, and have an absolute blast. They all were fond of cooking out, and I would take long dives in their swimming pool. We would do the same whenever we would go to Vermont. Dad was such a big fan of cooking out that he would set up a whole picnic in the yard. He would also take us hiking in the front yard and mountains. He would build a fire and cook smores, and I loved to enjoy swimming in the pond. A cousin I used to love spending time with would often show up as well every time I would visit with Dad. My dad would build us a tent outside the house, and my cousin and I would sleep outside in the tent. I loved to sleep in the tents. As a child, it had an extremely adventurous feel to it, and I wanted to consume it as much as I could. But that all changed as soon as the bugs started getting in. They had found a way to ruin my safe place.

Vermont's cold is different. The sheer ice-like amount of cold and the vast land-hiding snow they get in Vermont is mind-boggling. Like had it not been for cameras, maps and navigation systems, it would take little persuasion to convince me that Vermont is actually Antarctica. But hey, that's just me. However, such cold temperatures call for one thing for sure, if not another: A hearty breakfast. Dad, as he would always do, for my pleasure, took us to my favorite breakfast place: Hungry Bear in Vermont. I would always order French toast and orange juice for myself. Their syrup to put on the toasts was what made me their most loyal customer. I've yet to taste syrup like that anywhere else.

Dad's favorite way to pass his vacations every November was going up to Vermont and hunting deer. That's what he would say, but I know it was really going back to his family's home up there. It was the place where he was born and raised. I think it was revisiting his childhood memories in that home and everything he used to do as a child. It was his deer hunting stories, which he would tell about with so much excitement that I would just listen to him whenever he would share an anecdote. His eyes would become childlike and would exude so much excitement. I would generally not partake in cooking the deer meat or skinning the deer, but I would always sit there and listen to him talk about it when he came back. Just being there in his aura was my safe space.

On every Christmas I spent with Dad, I would get every wish I had on my list. On regular days, if I was sad for some reason, was just having a bad day or even if I was going through my menstrual cycle, he would always get me something to cheer my mood up, be it through a dessert or good ole' dollars. I remember when I found out I was pregnant at the age of 16, I was really depressed because I had to go through an abortion due to being pressured into one by my so-called family members and aunt. Even then, Dad would call an old friend of mine to our home and give me a few dollars to go shopping. He knew that going shopping takes my mind off of things. For me, it was his care that never let me turn over to the dark side. I know that he always knew that it never was going shopping, getting money, or being spoiled with love; it was just that my dad would do everything in his power to put a smile on my face when he knew I needed one the most or even if I didn't. He would always make sure that I remained in my happiest place. Perhaps he always believed that I had been dealt a pretty bad combination of cards in life and took it upon himself to raise me in the best circumstances. He would make sure that a smile never left my face.

As time went on and I got older, living with my aunt was becoming a hazard too much for me to bear. I mean… it took me some time to understand and come to terms with the fact that my aunt was a narcissist who was verbally, mentally and physically abusive. My dad knew it, of course, not that I would waste any chance to remind him that, but I could see it on his face whenever they would interact; his eyes would go down, and his face would be drained of any and all energy. Yet, whenever he would spend time with me, he would rejuvenate with the thrill of living. It's almost as if he saw something in me that transcends our concepts of living. It was in those little moments which seem like minute seconds when I reminisce on them now, but, even now, I know that every moment I spent with him carries within them the weight and value of entire lifetimes. Now, I just hope that he knows how much I cherish each moment I spent with him and that I will keep his memories for all of life and beyond, if there is one.

It was at the age of 20 that I realized how much our words and actions affect the ones who love us the most. One fine day, after waking up and brushing my teeth, I felt nauseous. At first, I didn't make much of it, but slowly, the symptoms started kicking in. I intentionally avoided Dad for a while so that I would not have to answer him and risk disappointment, especially in his eyes. I went to the doctor's for a check-up to confirm my suspicion. While I was at the clinic, my phone began to ring, and Dad was on the call. I answered his call and told him that I was at the doctor's, so I would call him back. To my surprise, the next question he asks is if I'm pregnant. I felt like this was the best moment to come clean to him. There would not, more so could not have been, be a better moment to break such news to him. As soon as I did, I could hear his voice breaking up; he was crying! I knew I had hurt him so much that it disappointed him to the core. I was 20 years old, old enough to make my own decisions. But the worst part of all of this fiasco for him was that my boyfriend at the time was the same guy who got his angel pregnant at the age of 16. He did not approve of him at all, probably because it didn't go well at all the last time it happened.

He did not oppose me keeping the baby. He even participated in all events leading up to my daughter's birth. Regardless of not liking the father of my child, it was my child nonetheless. There was no way Dad was going to miss out on something like MY first child being born. Just to showcase this man's love for me, I will let you know that when I was opening up the gifts of my baby shower, I received a gift from Dad as well. It was a baby shirt… MY baby shirt! It was the same shirt I came wearing from Colorado when I first moved back to Massachusetts. He had kept it all this time, and now, I would put the same shirt on my baby as well. If this is not love, I don't know what is. He has always remained a sweet and connected family man and it would show in moments of great deal about just how much he adored the ones he loved.

A few years later, I was blessed with the most amazing present for Dad, HIS FIRST GRANDSON! Even though he is not biological, he is his grandson regardless because I was the first to bring him one. He was supportive as always and was very happy for me to become a mother to a son. He still wasn't very impressed with my new boyfriend and father of my son. Some things don't change, I guess. But I know Dad was happy that his angel was happy. For him, that was all that mattered. It was because they were my children that Dad remained with them as their grandfather and treated my children like his own grandchildren, and, for me, that was more than enough that he would be there for me and my children.

Journey Through Life's Flow

The fondest memory for my son is when "Pa" would teach him how to play football. My son now plays as a quarterback for his high-school junior varsity team, and I know that Dad is in Heaven and super proud of him.

Three years later, when I was pregnant with my youngest daughter, again because of my turbulent relationship with my son's father, he was not ecstatic per se. All he ever wanted was the best for me, and I feel like he knew in one way or more that my relationship with my son's father was a ticking time bomb. Little did I realize the explosion of this explosive would take my relationship with Dad as collateral. The bond always remained. No one has nor ever can take Dad's place in my heart. But, after several unfortunate events and my decision to take time for myself, just like everybody else, I had less frequented my visits to him. *I miss him.* Do not get me wrong… I want nothing more than to look at him once more and let him know that his angel is doing just fine. Thank you… Dad.

From talking on the phone every day, sometimes, it got so bad that we would go weeks without talking at times. To make the family that I had now work and function and sustain, I burned every and all bridges, everything and people… I did not leave for myself a way back to the one who loved me, and that speaks volumes. He would always show up at my children's football and cheer practices and home games whenever he would visit home. He would always be in Charlestown for the events. Sometimes, he would show up even before us, and after the match, before going back home, we would stop by a pizza truck and get everything the children wanted for themselves. He also always kept his pocket full of Jolly Ranchers to give to the kids before we left to go back home after their practices or matches.

This man was not just an incredible father, brother, son and husband; he was also an amazing grandfather. And they loved him as much as their "Pa" loved them.

"Never missed anything" is an understatement, and do not ask the kids to ask him to be somewhere for them; he'd walk to wherever they asked him to if he didn't have a ride there… *This is not a drill!* Seriously. Birthday parties, baptisms, communions, surgical procedures, you name it… Dad was there. He would not miss a chance to support his own. That's the kind of man my dad was.

My dad had been sick for a few years, which I had known about. He was extremely sick and truly disliked living like that. The time that Dad would experience in those days was the most tough I've ever seen him in my whole life. He would be in constant pain because of his illness.

On April 4th, 2023, it was his birthday, and I tried calling him to wish him a happy birthday and have long conversations with him. But, for some reason, I could not get a hold of him. No one answered the phone. So, I thought of giving them some time and space… but in vain. Later that night, I got a call from my cousin-sibling. The news she gave me rocked my feet apart. *Dad is unresponsive and has been placed in a medically induced coma.* I lost all my senses; I couldn't feel a thing. My body went numb, and my brain stopped thinking. She informed me of a surgery that was to take place late in the night, or in the morning. I could only pray for my dad. Thankfully, the surgery went through, and Dad was recovering. All seemed to have been getting better, but later that same night, on April 5th, 2023, a father, grandfather, husband, son, savior, and noble gentleman took his final breaths amidst a family gathering that loved him and looked up to him. His final moments were that of love and compassion and peace… exactly what he deserved.

Sometimes, I miss him so much that I wish to sleep so that I can see him in my dreams. I have kept his picture as the wallpaper on my home screen. I like to take a look at him once a day at least… but now it's uncountable. I listen to one of his favorite songs *"Someone You Loved"* by Lewis Capaldi, just to feel close to him and his presence for a few minutes.

I love you, Dad. All the roses in the world!
~Love, Duke

Chapter 6

Aunt/Adopted Mom

And now, here we are. It is as bitter as it is necessary to tell you about how big of an influence my aunt/adopted mom had on my life decisions and me, personally. To be true to you, this is the chapter I dreaded doing the most. She's the one person who hurt me, hurled me, offered me away, intensified and validated the storm that had been brewing inside me throughout my life, from childhood to growing up and adulting… and not in a good way at all.

It doesn't always feel like that, though. Since I was a child, as in not even ten, she treated me well. She cared for me, combed my hair, cooked my favorite food, helped me dress up, played with me… basically, everything a child wants to do with their elder. She looked after me like I was her own baby. Everywhere she went meant I was with her. Even when she was in college, I was beside her during her classes.

During my visits to my real, actual and biological mom when she got out of jail, my aunt was where I felt the most comfortable: my safe space… for the time being. But… *My, Oh, my…* as I got older, I understood that life has a mischievous way of unraveling.

I lived in the Bunker Hill Projects in Charlestown, MA, as a kid. There came a time in the Bunker Hills when my aunt divorced Dad. I never understood how she could do that; I mean, she shouldn't have. Where else would she have found someone like him? After that, she started dating again. I never knew who was to blame for that. Don't get me wrong She eventually got pregnant and had my two younger siblings with her now husband, who is an amazing man, sweet man. We eventually moved out of the projects and moved to Somerville, MA, But that was too on a temporary basis because we soon moved back to Charlestown and lived in Mishawum Park for another few years before we moved into a cozy, warm and loving house in Revere, MA where I spent the end of grade school through high school before I moved out on my own at age 19.

By the time we had moved to Revere, that's when I felt like she had become someone else, as if she was not showing on her face what she was thinking in her mind because her words and actions didn't match anymore. Her attitude had also changed towards me, and for the worse. I had no memory of this woman. Honestly, to this day, I don't understand why. But it doesn't matter anymore; what's done is done. The past cannot be altered and shouldn't be by any means.

When we moved to Revere, I started to feel different; her treatment of me was different. Everyone, including my siblings, had rooms with heat ventilation, but for some ODD reason, my room was on the porch with a bunch of windows but no heat vents. At night, it used to get super cold. I had to make do with sleeping with the only blankets

I could find. Maybe not anymore, but as a child, getting ready for school in sheer cold. Eventually, *Thank God,* I was given a room in the house that was small (a bed, and a tall dresser were all that would fit); again no air vent for heating. But that was the shit, and I dealt with it. I'd complain, but it was what it was.

I always used to remind myself that she did a lot for me. She adopted me as an infant; I was sick and going through withdrawals and would always cry, according to her. When I was a teen, she would still take care of me, clothe me and feed me. She gave me shelter when she didn't have to, so I am extremely grateful to her. That's how I'd try to look at it. As an adult, I realized I was torturing myself. I would always get yelled at, but it was I who would always get the brunt of it all. Physically, mentally, and emotionally, I eventually became frustrated to the point that a rebellious fire slowly began to set ablaze within me. I became what you call an "out-of-control teen". I was so resentful because although she would yell and scream at my other siblings who lived with us, I felt like I got it the worst.

When she would go ahead and scold me without any regard that she was speaking to a human, her face rammed up right in front of me. Every word she spoke spewed literal spit. The poison from her tongue would spread into my blood vessels and clot me in places as to make the body collapse and faint there and then. It is not an experience I reminisce about fondly. Her words would cut so deep that it was impossible for me even to doubt that whatever she said was not intentional of how she truly felt. There were moments when I would ask her without voicing my confusion. *If you hate me so much, why did you keep me? Why take care of me? Why give me a motherly figure and then just suddenly stop being one?* So many things I wanted her to tell me, confront me and trust me, but she had built a wall against me that I had no idea how to bring down. It wasn't very good.

There were times when my anger would come out with her eldest child. Oh, did I become a monster in her eyes? Oh, yes. I felt like she despised me. She would not let a chance go to ridicule me and my mother, and often both. She screamed and cussed as she would lift me off of her daughter. She would tell me in those moments that I am an animal ... or crazy. Little did she realize that I was made to behave like one ... that I was left with no other way to show how I felt all the time: angry ... despised ... reckless ...infuriated ... miserable ... abandoned.

Her most notoriously famous comments, which she would pass on to me, were the taunts in which she compared me, my habits, my actions, and everything to my mother. "You're gonna be just like your mother!" Ohh that cut deep. That cut really deep! In her defense, she did not know that I was interpreting that she was reminding me who my mother was as if I needed any reminder and that I didn't think about it every day, every single moment. She would usually make that comment when she caught me doing things like smoking cigarettes. Mind you, they were only cigarettes. Never alcohol nor any other drugs, only cigarettes, but all she could see was my mother's image. Later on in life, when I grew the strength to look past her taunts and bitterness, I thought that maybe I was a reminder of her sister. Maybe the lady only needed an outlet to vent her steam. But! SHE SMOKED CIGARETTES, TOO!

She would always remind a girl who has lost both parents that she is a spitting image of her mother. While I admit that cigarettes are no way of healing, they only give you pain, which might help one take their mind off of a greater pain (like anti-venom); it only worsens the pain in the long run; she needn't say all the things she said. Regardless of how terrible my mother's life was and how naively dumb decisions she made, she is still my mother, the woman who brought me, my beautiful sister, Alicia, and my brother into the world. Despite my love for my aunt for all the things she did for me, I can't get past her actions and words without blaming her a little. I just can't.

Her constant reminder of my past life would take me back there. The painful and tragic life with my family. The constant crying, screaming, perpetual uncertainty as to what's going to happen the next day. I had vowed, even as a child, that I would never let myself go back to that place mentally or emotionally. I was livid. It does not take much to predict what a teenager would do if they are put in a place where they do not want to be. I screamed, I smashed, I lashed at anyone whom I could get my hands on, which generally was my eldest cousin, my aunt's eldest child. She would tease just a little, and I would pop! My aunt would scramble to save her from me. I was termed as the angry one, but after a point, I stopped caring what they thought of me. I became irrational. It was the worst when she raised her hands at me because I wouldn't stop myself from retaliating. Yeah, that's how bad it would get; my aunt and I were throwing hands at each other. I was done with her keeping me as her punching bag, which she would use whenever she felt that life was not going her way. She would project all her insecurities on me, scream at me, call me names, and hit me. Frankly, I have no remorse that I fought back.

After my childhood and up until I reached young adulthood, I never heard an affectionate or endearing word for me from her mouth. I don't mean to take her credit away from her where she deserves it. She was nice to me at times when she would ask me late at night if I had eaten anything. There were times when she showed that she truly was my aunt and did care for me. But, all those times, it felt made up or even fake. It was as if she was trying to be someone else. Maybe to tell others in the vicinity that she isn't this terrible person whom I know about, or maybe to tell me in a way that it wasn't always her dark side that I had to deal with. Perhaps she was only convincing herself. I guess we will never know. There are moments that I cannot forget about, regardless of how much I get angry at her ... when I was in labor. She always showed up. That was a time when I needed someone to be with me, as all women who are beginning their motherhood journey do. She was always there with me during that painful but beautiful moment of giving birth. I could've never fought that. But she let someone throw a soda cup by my child. Now that I can't let it pass.

When I became a mother, it became more apparent that she treated my children differently at times than her own grandchildren. I mean, yeah ... they are her own children's children, but so were I and my children, so she'd say let the other children stay overnight at her place but not mine. Not my son. Only my girls. She would say that he was "too much" for her, whereas it was her children, my sibling, who got into an argument with me over my children's father and quickly heated things up. She was so livid about it that she threw a Burger King cup of soda across the living room when my daughter was right there. It could've hit her. I think mothers can relate that whoever tries to get at my children, I will rip them open. Not my babies. Guess what happened next ...

It was an all-out war between me and the sibling in question. In no time, I was on top of the sibling, pulling her hair and throwing hands. My aunt was doing her best to pull me off of her and kept calling me crazy and an animal. She did succeed, but can you believe her?! She didn't even bother to know why we were fighting, only that I was the animal and her daughter was my prey. I stopped granting them even a thought after that. I was done. Even up till a year ago, she still can't spare two cents for my sake. Trust me, I checked. I went to her to be consoled. I know I know ... *I can't believe I put myself in such a position!*

After my break up with my boyfriend of 15 years, I went to her to speak my heart out, naively thinking that she would be a listening ear. When I told her about all that had happened between us, her initial and only response was, "Oh, get over it already! I told you that you should've left a long time ago." I mean ... WHAT?! I knew it was up to me to take charge of my happiness. After reconciling with myself and subjugating my emotional turmoil, I needed to go out and achieve something. So, I joined a modeling agency that also offered placements in acting gigs. I was accepted as an emerging talent. I was ecstatic. Finally, something that I had achieved on my own. It wasn't like I made it into Hollywood, but I had been selected somewhere based purely and solely on my own accord and hard work. Maybe, if I bring her some good news, she would be happy for me, maybe not as much as I would be, but somewhat. This time, the shame was actually on me, as they say in that proverb. She asked me to confirm with them if they're legit. This time, I did see how I brought it onto myself. So I was hoping that I had learned the lesson now, that the moment when we desire validation from others for our own happiness is the point beyond which we have forsaken growth. All I could think about then was, *Aunt, why didn't you congratulate me? Are you not surprised that I did it? Finally, achieved something?* It was the best thing after my children to happen to me to date, and I had thought ill of it because my aunt wasn't as ecstatic as I am; in fact, quite the contrary.

This all reminded me of the time when I graduated high school. Perhaps that's just my inner child talking, but having watched others celebrate their high-school graduations, I had hoped I would at least get a gift. Well … there was no party, no gift, not even a fuckin' card … pardon my French. It was like nothing I'd ever do would be enough for her, always taunting me, ridiculing my existence, and thinking ill of me. Nothing would ever make her believe that I was capable of good, let alone be proud of me. Later into my adult life, I have grown distant from her, loving from afar. I let her attend to her life as I cater to mine.

When Dad died in April of 2023, she sought me out and offered to meet again after such a long time. At first, I was hesitant, but then I entertained the thought that perhaps this was an opportunity … to let off what I had thought about all this time for my childhood, my adult life, my aunt … to finally be able to get it off of my chest all the pain that I had borne all this time. Another reason to meet her, which was a much bigger reason, was that I believed it might make Dad happier, and that was it. I was meeting her.

When we did meet, she was so, so happy to see me. She reached out to give me a hug and kiss as soon as we came in touching distance. When we did, she pulled back, looked me in the eye, and told me, "She missed me." I know! I was thinking the same thing! "Who are you, and where is my aunt?!" We went inside and sat for a while. It was then that I decided I needed to rip open the band-aid. In my defense, what was to come next, she had pre-approved by saying that she was open to talking about our shared past. Then, I began conversing about Mom. I asked her why she told me that Mom had given away her rights to me, and that is why she was never there for me. I wanted to cut in deep and unravel the answers to questions I had in my mind since childhood. But, her response was so miserly, "I never said that she loved you. I don't recall saying that to you … ever." I call *Bullshit!* She wouldn't break that easy. I brought the question to her about the treatment that she would bestow on me, telling everybody that I was an angry menace. I went on to explain to her why I was so angry and damned mad all the time and how she had a huge role to play in it. Of course, she denied all of it, saying, "I never did that," and, "I never said that, I don't recall that."

I was tired of listening to her lies and denying everything I was throwing at her. I realized that she is not going to admit her faults and mistakes. So, I left it to God and let her know I did. I told her, "God hears all and sees all. One day, you are going to have to answer to him about all that you have done, so, goodluck. He can and will deal with you."

After all that has happened with and between my aunt and me, I have chosen to stay away and love her from afar, whatever I can, that is. I do not wish to be in her presence, nor do I have any wish to involve her in my life. I am and will always remain grateful for what she has done for me. Raising me, sheltering me, feeding me, and giving me a motherly figure when I had even started despising the thought of the image in my mind. Thank you, Auntie. But, truth be told, I do not wish her any bad; I forgive her, and I wish that I never have to see her again.

Chapter Seven

Friendships and Relationships

"The meeting of two personalities is like the contact of two chemical substances: if there is any reaction, both are transformed."

~Carl Jung

Relationships and friendships, or all kinds of bonds for that matter, have always been a case of curiosity to me. Maybe it has to do with my lack of experience of a true and "come-what-may" kind of relationship except with my dad. Otherwise, my social ventures, especially romantic pursuits, have almost always been just that … incomplete.

Loving is a part of my nature. I believe in a loving world, and despite being exposed to a world where being kind is considered naïve, I believe love will make space for all of us to live in harmony. So that is what my demeanor is and what my personality comprises. But again and again … and again, I had been treated to the same outcome: I love them and care for them, and they betray and leave me. I found myself subjected so many times to gaslighting and manipulation. Until the point when I decided to burn all bridges and look after my own mental health, I had put myself in a position where I had given others the power to decide what was better for me and what was not.

As a child, I would make a lot of friends. Growing up and meeting children from different households in school, it was as easy as it is for a child to have fun with other kids. But, it's only after one grows up that they realize that friendships and genuine relationships are one, if not the most, rare blessings in life. Having lived the life I have lived, I got to learn early in life how opportunist the world is. And being as naïve as I was, I did not listen to or analyze my elders' experiences and was left at the mercy of life to teach me all these important lessons about living ... and let me just tell you, life is one cruel teacher, but it makes sure you learn.

I had friends throughout my elementary, middle school, and high school years. As I grew up, my circles became smaller and smaller. It was perhaps because I had learned how to distinguish between who had my best interest at heart and who was the imposter. It was during the times when I was in my two prominent relationships, and these are the ones from which my children were born. I would ask my friends for advice about what to do during the dark days in my love life, which I have had my fair share. They would always suggest to me what they thought was best, but they didn't know how I felt; they could've never known. I would take their advice to heart. Perhaps it was the fact that I only sought comfort in conversing with them. What I did not realize was that I, over time, became so overly reliant on their advice and wisdom that I never built my own. It was not until later on in my life that I understood that when confronting a problem, my friends wouldn't be there to protect me. I will have to do that on my own, and for that, I had to start believing in myself and my own understanding. All this time of believing that someone else knows better for me than I do had to change.

I had always been extremely co-dependent and wanted someone to always be around me. So, I kept friends around me all the time. I did not like being alone. I mean … who does? But, even after resorting to solitude for as far as I want to think back, sometimes, I, too, blur the lines between solitude and loneliness. Anyways, the child in me could've never learned the term solitude, let alone fathomed the concept of it. I would also jump from relationship to relationship, trying to find a potential suitor. Well, I didn't find what I was looking for, but abandonment issues did find their way to me. So much that they made a home in me, and they flourished until I put a stop to them after my last relationship crumbled to shambles. That is when I forced myself to burn bridges and let myself heal.

My first significant relationship was with my oldest daughter's father. I was sixteen years old then. I had seen him while visiting an old friend. I found him quite cute, so I had to go through a family friend to get a chance to get in touch with him. We did and hung out soon after. It was like a thunderbolt had struck me. I cannot describe the kind of butterflies I was experiencing then. I was certain, at least at that moment, that it was love at first sight. At that time, it had felt like a fairytale come true. All that I had thought until then, that I had been good to everyone, so only the best would happen to me, was turning out to be true. I was extremely excited, but just within the month, I would get to know the dreaded news. I was pregnant. I know … I know. We were way too young. At first, I had wanted to keep the baby. So, I called the only person I had hoped would understand what I was going through … Mom, my biological mom. She did … she did understand me.

She came and picked me up from the train station because my aunt wasn't in agreement with my initial decision. She was as excited as I am and even offered to support me through this time by taking care of her baby and her baby's baby as well. But after having grown-up conversations with Mom, I realized the importance of graduating before I could go ahead and take on the responsibility of parenting. As much as I wanted to be a mother, I could not condone the fact that I had to finish my studies in order to support and sustain a household.

After deciding to go through with the abortion, I broke up with him. I was in a turmoil of emotions. I was all over the place. I was in even greater shock when I found out that he was having twins with someone else. I was devastated, but perhaps I had already gone through much worse previously that I found it easier to move on from. I believe my life experiences have left behind a personality, a mind, a heart, and a spirit that is capable of thinking differently, enduring incredibly, and forgiving mercilessly. After four years of going through all that I had with my family, or whatever was left of it, I met him again.

We began living together now that we were both consenting adults. He treated me like a queen, buying me flowers damn near every day, always cleaning and he even bought me my first dog. We would spend all the time with each other, and within a month … I was pregnant. But this time, I wanted to have the baby. I was ready to be a mother. Oh my, I was excited. I had a job that was going by smoothly; I had money coming into the account regularly. I had an apartment I was renting; it was a cool spot, and, most importantly, he was on board as well. We both were so excited to begin a journey of our own. But that excitement was to be short-lived because, the day after we learned that we were expecting, I heard a knock on the door—a loud thumping. It was the cops. They came with a warrant for him. They took him and put him in jail, and I was evicted, shortly later, out of my apartment. The case of why they took him to jail is less important. It was what happened after rather than before. It is almost always the cause that we must worry about more than the effect. Anyhow, he remained locked up for most of the duration of my pregnancy. Even after all that time, had I not bailed him out, I didn't know when he'd have ever gotten out. My reason for bailing him out was not only that I was so madly in love with him, but that I didn't want to go through it on my own. As a matter of fact, I did just that. For the part of pregnancy when he was not there and after my eviction, I had to take care of myself on my own. Those sleepless nights were emotionally and mentally some of the toughest ones I had faced. The difference between this pain and all the others was that it was worth it on the other side with this one. Motherhood is truly a transcendental experience. But until I was a mother, it was a shit show. I bailed him out because it was important for my daughter to see her father as she was being born. It was so important that I gave my daughter a whole family feeling when she was born. It was even more important for me.

I called him, trying for hours, and told him I was in labor and needed him to come as quickly as he could. He arrived a few minutes after I had given birth. For seven months of my pregnancy, I had worked and saved enough money to bail him out. I had poured in my tireless effort, insomniac state of mind, and literal blood and sweat, even went into pre-term labor on the job, just for him to miss the most important moment of my child's life. But, even though he was late, he was there. He came through, and that's what I'm most glad about.

For most of the duration of my pregnancy, I stayed with my older sibling. After the birth of my eldest daughter, I stayed there, at my sibling's place, until she was five months old. This was due to two major reasons, among others: First, her father not being able to come by often and help out with baby things. I didn't want to do everything on my own. It is important for my child to have more than one elder, and second, I no longer felt comfortable there.

My daughter's father stayed with me the whole time in the hospital after he showed up. He would do everything from running and bringing any food or medication we needed to check up with the doctors if we needed anything and when we could be discharged. He would even come by every day from morning to night after we went from the hospital to my sibling's house. He would come by to my sibling's house and barely put our daughter down. He was absolutely elated to have his daughter in his arms all day long. I give credit where it's due regardless of how I feel about them in real life. My daughter's dad was an absolute gem of a father. He played with her, bathed her, fed her, and at night, after feeding her and putting her to bed, he would leave and come back the next day.

After a month or two, my sibling developed an urge to hate my daughter's father. She began disliking the very core of him. In my opinion, she had grown jealous of him because her partner was barely around to help with her children.

I felt that way because neither of her children's fathers were around. I had snuck him in a few times because it was winter, and I had a newborn whom I wasn't taking out in the cold so she could have a bond with her father. And no offense, but I shouldn't have had to. He wasn't doing anything wrong but trying to be a father. So what was really the problem? Maybe she wanted me to be a single mother like everyone else. By the time our daughter was four to five months, he was seeing her maybe once or twice a week, to fewer and fewer as time went on. Our relationship even dwindled by that time also. We eventually broke up due to cheating, lying, no help with our daughter, and betrayal! After having our daughter, I got my taxes. Five thousand dollars. He told me prior to our breakup that he found us an apartment. So I gave him the money, my whole refund for the apartment, and he decided to go on a shopping spree and spend my money all the more. So yes, obviously, he lied. He left our baby and me with just about eighty dollars. After everything, feeling broken, hurt, lied to, cheated on, and betrayed in the worst way, I went into a shelter with my baby so I could rebuild my life.

While in the shelter, the disrespect continued. He was seeing this one girl, and this girl called my phone one day to let me know who she was with and called me "homeless". Evidently, she didn't know that I was put out because of him. During the time of me being in the shelter, I focused on my mental health and worked on being a great young mom, making memories upon memories with my baby. I ended up moving on with my life and started dating again. I eventually got my own apartment again. The guy I was dating at the time was the person I was seeing when I was 14 years old; he was 22 years old. We first met one day when I was out with a friend. We were downtown, walking through the Boston Commons. They were having the "Walk for Hunger'" and we didn't know what it was or what it was about. So we went to go and check it out. While walking through the Commons, he was at first sitting on a bench with two guys and a baby. He walked over to me and started talking. We eventually exchanged numbers and met up a day or two later. After talking on the phone and spending time with each other, he eventually told me he was married, but they were "separated". He also told me he lived with his mom, so I didn't mind giving him a chance. We hung out often, multiple times a week. He'd come to see me while I was working and also after work. We would speak on the phone all the time if we weren't in each other's face. We even planned to have kids during one of the times we were hanging out. We were at "Revere Beach" sitting on the wall, and I pointed at the doctor's office across the street and said, "Yup, and I'll go there for my prenatal visits."

After a few months of talking and hanging out, spending time being intimate, you name it, we eventually broke things off. I caught him in a lie. One day, he called me, and I heard his kids in the background. He tried to say he was watching them, but something about what he was saying felt off; I felt that he and his wife were together, and I was coming in between people. So, I left him alone. I knew he was still, in fact, married and living with her. He attempted to talk to me again a few years later while in a relationship with someone else. I had been living on my own at that point in my first apartment. He came by with his younger brother and others; while we were talking, I asked him if he was single, and that's when he told me he was in a relationship. I then showed him the door. Honestly, I just felt like I was too good to lower myself to even entertain that. While I was in the shelter, his brother came out while I was visiting my older sibling. Well, he came along too. I hadn't seen him in over a year or two, and by that time, I had my daughter and had broken up with her dad. So this time, I decided to finally entertain him again. And he was single. When I got my second apartment while being in the shelter, we decided to move in together. During our living together in the beginning and even while I was in the shelter, he was talking to other women, but I brushed it aside. I just wanted to believe that he loved me and my daughter, so I swept it under the rug because he kept saying he didn't want them and would cut them off. Everything between us was okay for a while. We started to try and really work on things by hanging out and stuff. We also decided to start a family together. So, about a year into us being together, living together with my daughter, I found out I was pregnant, and we were both so excited and seeing how great he was with my daughter, I knew we were moving in the right direction. Well, that was short-lived because I eventually found out he cheated on me with a coworker while I was pregnant with our son as a "BET!" I was devastated. He decided to make it up to me by proposing to me. At that point. I thought we were finally going to do things the right way. We have our family now we're planning marriage. well, that didn't quite happen because after our son was born, he started with the in and outs. I'd catch him cheating; I'd put him out. He'd beg, plead, and even threaten to end his life. I'd take him back, and the cycle would continue. We eventually moved. A few months to a year later, I found out I was pregnant yet again. This time with our daughter. His first girl. So to me, I thought things were getting better. We were living the life we manifested when we first met. Well, that wasn't gonna happen. Happy family, marriage, new apartment. NOPE! What did happen was while I was pregnant with our daughter, his first daughter, I caught him cheating again. This time with our children's daycare teacher. What the fuck?! I was infuriated, like what is the problem? Why aren't we enough? So, I spent most of my pregnancy alone. About a month before I gave birth, he called me on New Year's Day ... drunk in the morning in shambles. Crying about how he's such a bad person, how I'm giving him his first daughter, sorries, him just wanting his family back, he's ready to come home and do right by us, he doesn't want to miss the birth of our daughter. So, AGAIN ... I took him back. Everything was going well. I gave birth to our daughter; he was there. Damn near missed the birth, though, because he went to get something to eat. I kept trying to call his phone, but he didn't answer. So I said, "Fuck it," and started pushing. He ended up walking in during my pushing. Our daughter was born, and he was in awe of her. But, as always, that was short-lived. He supposedly went on a "cruise" a few months after the birth of our daughter with his cousin. What he didn't realize was that I knew how it went. He needed a passport! Something he didn't have. But he insisted he was good with or without one. Well, we fought, he left and disappeared for two weeks. After coming back weeping, begging and crying again, admitting how he's such a bad man, he's so sorry he doesn't know why he keeps doing the shit he keeps doing; he just wants his family back. All the same old shit he always says anytime he fucks up. Come to find out, he was with a woman for those two weeks.

I was so mad, but I still just wanted to give my children what we didn't have … a home, a family they came from, and of course, because I loved him, I took him back. So, as always, things were good for a while. He'd try to "prove" himself and how much he cared/loved me by buying me things and taking me on dates, being affectionate, watching movies, giving quality time, calling all the time when he's at work, then it's the same song and dance. He'd get distant, he picks a fight so he can leave for however long he wants, cheats; that doesn't work out, so he calls and begs me to come back; I come back, he loves bombs, and then the cycle continues. As time went on, I started to wake up and catch on to what was truly going on. This wasn't love at all; in fact, it was damn near abuse. It was toxic, it was hurtful, and it was embarrassing if I'm being honest. Embarrassing to who? Myself. But at that point in time in my life, I didn't know my worth or what I deserved. I was used to everyone in my life using me and taking me for granted, so shit, it was normal. Until I really got tired of it and not just from him, but from EVERYONE, friends, family, you name it. But I kept on what I call "the" hamster wheel of my situationship because it wasn't LOVE, not even close. So, a few years later, I decided while I was working that things weren't working out, but we stayed together. While working, I met someone and really liked him. So, I eventually emotionally cheated for a while. This person made me feel what I hadn't felt in years … SEEN. He would notice everything about me. My kid's father no longer paid attention to me. His hugs felt so comforting. I actually felt cared about for once. But I decided to leave that job for a better one, so that situation stopped. Honestly, I did it partially because I wanted him (my children's father) to get a taste of his own medicine and thought it would open up his eyes and stop hurting me, but it didn't. It was actually something for him to now use as amo to throw in my face whenever I would bring up his cheating. During our relationship, my older sibling accused him of something that he was later found guilty of, so he wasn't working because finding and keeping a job was impossible for him. So, I became the main breadwinner while I was working by myself to support our family, making sure our bills were paid, making sure we had the best of the best materialistically, making sure we had the money for our weed habit, his drinking and cigarette habit, the kids have what they want and need. I caught him on numerous occasions receiving money from other women. I was FURIOUS!!! How demeaning and disrespectful can you be? It's like no amount of money or love was ever enough for this dude! My eyes began to open up about what I was dealing with. I eventually started to really wonder what was happening. Our arguments started to become physical on both ends but mainly mine. I could talk and talk to get him to understand how he was making me feel, but it's like he didn't give a shit. I would cry, scream, yell, and he wasn't fazed at all, not even a little bit. So I figured and would always say, "If he doesn't hear my words, then he's gonna feel these hands."

I must say, it's a part of my life I'm the most disappointed in myself about. Nor am I proud. But while going through things with him, I felt like I was going crazy. I'd ask him about cheating, talking to other women, or getting money from them; he'd deny and make excuses, deflect the accusation and blame me, and call me crazy and insecure. If I found evidence, he'd tell me I didn't see what I had seen, or he'd put it on me because I went searching. After googling what I was going through because I couldn't take it anymore, I learned that I was dealing with a "NARCISSIST". Once I did my research on the topic, everything started to make sense.

Not only was he one, but some of my family members are or show traits of it, most importantly my aunt. She was my first encounter. I knew because of all of the things he would say, kind of like, throw a rock, hide your hand. And make you feel crazy for calling them out on it. People who I thought were friends too. It all started to make sense to me. So, I began to look at everyone around me differently. Now that I know what I'm dealing with, I can't unsee it. When I lost my sister, he was basically the only one who I "thought" was there for me. No one really called and checked on me all but one friend. She knew what I felt because she had lost a sibling, too. But what he would do when I was grieving was point out the fact that nobody was there. He'd always say when I was at my lowest, "See, nobody gives a fuck about you. I'm the only one still here. They ain't calling or coming to see you. I'm the only one putting up with you." Although he was somewhat right, maybe it was still hard. When I went through my miscarriage again, I felt alone. I was devastated because it was something again I "thought" we both wanted. I struggled to realize I was grieving another loss on my own. I'd cry and cry and cry, and he'd just watch me unfazed and emotionless.

One time, while I was super emotional about it, he came and tried to hug me while I was crying. I told him to let me go, and he just walked away. Once I gathered myself, I came into our bedroom, and he was lying with one foot on the bed, looked at me and said, "You done crying now?" I couldn't believe my ears when he said it. Like wow, you really don't give fuck about me or what I'm going through! My love for him really started to fade, and I started to want to leave him alone more and more because I already felt alone. My last straw was back in 2022 when one day, he was just going back and forth to the "liquor store" all day long, but he had no money and would come back empty-handed. So I questioned it, and as always, he gave me excuse after excuse as to why he would come back with nothing. So, during the day, one of my younger siblings was here, and we were talking about sexual things. Well, he joined in the conversation and made a sexual comment about one of my siblings. I was in complete shock and pissed at the same time. It just added to the hurt I had already felt. The disrespect I already felt. Normally, I'd kick him out, but this time, I sat and stewed in those thoughts and feelings I felt. which was unusual for me. I'd normally react off of impulse, but I didn't. After a few days of sitting and pondering on how I was feeling and what was said, I had had it. Everything I had been through ran through my mind, good things and bad. But what I realized is during this relationship, I computely lost myself. My confidence, self-esteem, love for myself, how I had seen myself, and what I felt about myself. It got so low. Low enough that I became suicidal.

My weed habit, which I had never had my whole life, was at an all-time high. I know this was "DONE". I was DONE! So one night while I was at work, I thought to myself, it's either him or ME. Well, I chose me!

So I woke up the next day and decided to put him out for the last time. I had officially had enough after 15 years of what felt like complete and utter HELL. I was done and had nothing left to give. And what's crazy is how his ex-wife one day, early in our relationship while on the phone, told me how he'd leave me with kids, debt, and needing to have a therapist on speed dial. Well, she wasn't wrong. Matter of fact, she was spot on. When I put him out, I was left in hundreds of dollars of debt, car insurance not paid, bills getting cut off, left to provide for my kids by myself, broken-hearted, damaged mentally and emotionally. I had to go on medical leave from work because I was suicidal and felt alone and over life.

Everything with him, family, friends all the trauma I experienced came to me and hit me like a ton of bricks. My whole life kept playing in my head like a movie. A nightmare, actually. All my abandonment issues were coming up, all my past negative experiences were coming up, and I couldn't run from it this time around. I started to realize that in my past, I'd jump from relationship to relationship. Always have friends and family around, so I didn't have to face my trauma. This time around, that wasn't the case. A few months prior to the breakup, I stopped talking to my friends and family, so it was like I had nobody but my kids. I felt I had no one.

At this point in my life, I had no choice but to face myself. I knew I couldn't run from ME anymore. It was so bad that smoking weed no longer helped. It actually made what I was feeling ten times worse. I was no longer eating or sleeping. All I did was cry all day, every day. I lost a ton of weight. Well, during the relationship, I gained, at one point, over 60 pounds; well, I lost all that. I truly felt like I was going crazy inside. I just wanted out. Out of life, out of it all. When I went on leave from work, I gave myself one month to get myself together. To get all the crying and frustration out, but most importantly, to finally allow myself to start healing. Healing recent and past wounds. Especially the ones I had pushed deep, deep down.

Honestly, I feel that losing my sister, my miscarriage, and this breakup served for me as a catalyst for my spiritual awakening. I feel like that because I was at a terrible place in my life. Heavily consumed weed on the regular, stayed extremely depressed, pushed everyone away because I no longer trusted anyone, and was just over life all too much. I most definitely was down and out. I was crushed and felt, LITERALLY, defeated. But not for long ...

Chapter Eight

My Children

This next chapter is the one that I have looked forward to the most. I am so excited to tell you guys about my three blessings. About the three angels who have made my life worth living, who have made me want to get out of bed in the mornings, I had found a happy place of my own, made me feel loved and the most accepted and cared about.

Leading this list is my firstborn. On Christmas Day, God bestowed upon me one of the greatest blessings that he could've ever given me and the one that I could have ever received. My time in labor had been quite stressful; I was both emotionally and physically completely exhausted. However, I will always maintain that it was so worth it in the end. When I found out that I was pregnant with her, I did not know what to make of it. I had mixed feelings. I had both anxiety and extreme excitement, and all I knew was that my life was going to change … completely. As soon as I felt her inside my womb, I knew that I would never remain the same person I had been.

Giving birth to her was one of the greatest and the most euphoric moments of my life. While I was in labor,

Christine Pimental

I was told that the umbilical cord had been wrapped around her neck and it was choking her, so they had me lay from side to side in order to release pressure off of her neck and off of the cord. And if that didn't work, then I would have had to go in for an emergency C-section. This made me panic so much, and at that moment, I was going out of my mind. The only thought that was going in my head was about my child. I could not lose her. Not then. Not now. Not ever.

But I could feel that I was protected that day, and, by the grace of God, I made it to ten centimeters, and when I was ready to push, my baby came out. A beautiful, healthy, and adorably cute baby. From the first looks, she looked pissed, to be honest, but that was just her face … I'm kidding! I was so excited and felt so blessed that I cried out of joy, and tears streamed down my face when they finally put her on my chest. It was official: I was a mom. It was at that moment I realized something I had never known throughout my life. I had always believed that I wanted and needed someone to love me and take care of me. Turns out, having her in my arms, on my chest, looking up at me and me looking down at her, I realized that all I ever wanted was to love someone so much and so completely that they couldn't have enough, and for them to love me back with as much genuineness. That's all. And on that Christmas Day, I received my best Christmas present ever.

Journey Through Life's Flow

After we were discharged from the hospital, my daughter and I went back to my older siblings' house, and we stayed there for a few months. We had. But when my baby was about five months old, I made the decision to go into a shelter program so that I could start building a new life of my own and provide the best for this beautiful blessing that I had found to properly bring the foundation for us, from which we could start afresh, lead a healthy, comfortable and wholesome life. It was during those times that things started to fall apart with her father. And eventually I decided to go at this alone and raise my daughter on my own.

Going into the shelter program was scary, and I was truly afraid. In the shelter programs, you're around a bunch of people that you don't know, so how can you know who to trust? But my daughter and I ended up meeting some really cool and sweet people. Maybe God was looking out for us after all. I also learned a lot during the process. Initially, sometime during the day, I would go out and hang out with my relatives. But soon enough, I realized that I was only running away from my new reality by doing so. I knew that I needed to sit down and face what I had chosen and to live up to the decision that I had made. So, one day, I decided to stay in and face what our new life had become, even though I knew that it was all temporary and had to change at some point, but it was very real. I knew that I needed to learn how to be independent.

It was stressful, difficult, and sometimes crumbling, but it was a beautiful time in our lives as we made a bunch of memories together. I would take my daughter out to a nearby water park, and I would be completely amazed by how happy my daughter was just by being in that place and having fun on her own. She was only a few months old at this point, so I know that she didn't really care for what was going on around her. Seeing her in this blissful happiness was something that I had cherished in my childhood, and I had always thought that I would see in myself again. What I didn't know was that I would see myself in my daughter someday. And it was some moment. To see her enjoy the small measures of happiness in life, was always beautiful. I also knew that she was young and that, at this time in her life, she probably wouldn't remember. And that's how I wanted it. I only wanted the best for her. I had to start now. I had to go out, and I had to teach my daughter how to be a strong, powerful and independent woman.

During the night times, sometimes, when I would let her stay up a little more, we would sit in the room and listen to music, especially the song I dedicated to her, "No One" by Alicia Keys. It was so soothing and so tranquil. But she was there, and still is, to this day, my comfort zone. Seeing her cute little face every day, looking so innocent and naive and remaining unfazed by this new reality, that I had chosen for me and my daughter. Her high spirits kept my spirits up, and seeing her enjoy the little things in life helped me stay motivated. All I knew in those trying times was that as long as we had each other, nothing else mattered.

I would be sitting in the chair, and would be running my fingers through her head. Just looking at her was a joy of life that I did not want to miss. I would kiss her cute little face while hugging her in the tightest embrace, and truth be told, sometimes I would shed a tear as well. Still, to this day, on some occasions or at family events, I play this. Theme song for her. And the girl knows all the words!

While we were living in the shelter, I had my eyes on something else; my goal was to spend the coming Christmas together … in our own home …. Come December 1st, we were moving into our first home together! It was just like I wanted it to be. It came right in time for her 1st birthday. This was one of the greatest achievements I have had in life. I was so proud and happy and felt so accomplished. It was great to have that experience because it was something after which I felt life could take a much better turn, and we could move further ahead as a family.

The birthday party was incredible. It was our first Christmas together; it was her first birthday as well. I had chosen a Winnie the Pooh theme for her birthday party. She loved Winnie, and all of our family and friends … at least most of them … were there to help celebrate.

Christine Pimental

Frankly, I must admit here. But for the longest while, it always made me sad that her biological father was never in attendance for any of her birthday parties and later down the line, even at her cheering competitions, even though he was always invited. And it really annoyed me, but more importantly, hurt me and I know it eventually hurt her too.

If I am to tell you about my dear daughter, my fashionable diva, that's what I used to call her Growing up and still to this day. She loved dressing up, and in her childhood, she would dress up as a Disney Princess and she would put on their dresses with matching heels. She just likes to dress up. She always has, and still does, to this day. She's quite fashionable and very confident, perhaps one of the most adorable qualities that I love the most.

When she got to the age where she was able to start school, I was super emotional. My baby was growing up in front of my eyes. And now she would be away. I was so not ready for this. The day I dropped her off to school on her first day of kindergarten. I am not ashamed to admit ... I wailed. In her first grade, I chose to sign her up for cheerleading. And she would cheer for my home, town of Charlestown, MA. I was so proud of my baby. Her facials, a genuine talent at cheering. She was always on point ... always has been. Then, since she started, her moves have always been on point as well. It's like she's performing, and she loves it. Watching her cheer was always. A proud moment for me, and it always brought me so much joy.

Especially during our competitions, I felt like I was the loudest, proudest mom in the gym. She would hit every stunt to the point and again, those expressions had the most charisma.

Her mannerisms and the way she carries herself, it has taught me so much and brought about a better version of me. She truly has a heart of gold. But she also has a no-nonsense type of mindset. I call her my little Pitbull. Because she's always very sweet, super sweet, in fact, but then again, she will take no nonsense from anyone. Friends, family. She doesn't care. And I love that about her. She is very protective of me. And also her siblings. She is the eldest and she shows that in herself. She is a very loving human, but her love, it's tough love sometimes. She definitely has no problem saying what is on her mind, and she is unapologetically authentic. Respectfully, of course. She is a teen now, and soon to legally be an adult. It is even crazy that I'm saying that. I can't believe my little baby will go out in the world independently and be independent. Whereas it was actually something that she taught me: independence, maturity and strength. In a way, I had her when I was young, in my early 20s, so she was basically growing up with me and we were growing up together by helping each other. She, by no stretch of the imagination, is my little best friend.

We talk about everything and anything. As a young girl, I have always raised her with the awareness that she could talk to me about anything and there was nothing that she could not discuss with me. It is something that I was never able to feel with my aunt when I was growing up. That was always something I had wished that whenever I became a mother and had my own children, I would make sure that they would be completely frank with me, honest to me, and true to me. They would talk to me about anything and they would feel safe around their mother. I've always been determined to raise my children how I wish I had been. And it all starts with open communication. And it began with her. She was the one who taught me how to be a better person. Oh, boy … she talks, and I love it, so I let her for the most part. She's very open with me; I love that. And love that we help each other through different issues or matters that are going on in our lives.

When I was pregnant with her, I was severely sick. I had had a really bad morning sickness, but, truth be told, it was an all-day sickness. Everything I smelled made me throw up. I worked throughout my pregnancy but had to go on leave early because I worked with food, and I would throw up on the job, especially when I was handling the food. When I went back after being out for a month, I would go to work for a few more months. I had a stomach ache, or so I thought. But during my shift, when I was working with a coworker, she noticed I wasn't myself. She eventually asked me if I was okay. I told her yeah. But that I had woken up with a stomach ache; she continued to watch me and, eventually, told me that I needed to go upstairs to labor and delivery because something didn't feel right. So she walked up there with me, and within an hour or two of being seen, I found out that I was in preterm labor. I remained in the hospital for a few days so that they could watch me and stop my contractions. Eventually, days later, I was able to go home but had to remain on bedrest to properly recover. So, I quit working because I had used up most of my maternity leaves. No regrets!

This is my most favorite chapter to write in this book because becoming a mother was something I had wanted to experience since I was a child. I wanted to become a mom because I always wanted someone to love and someone to love me back. I knew that I had so much love to give, but more importantly, I could love my children the way I wanted to be loved in my own childhood. My children are my everything. They are my whole world. They are the very reason that I get up every day and never give up. They are why I look at life from a different perspective. The love that I have for my children is like no other I have ever felt. I feel like it can overwhelm them at times. As if it's too much for them, and they feel their teenage rebellion coming about. But I just never want them to ever have to question how I feel for them.

Having my three beautiful blessings gave me a sense of purpose in life to go on and live and work and become a great role model because someone was depending on me. It wasn't always like that. I did feel that I had put myself on a pedestal, but I realized later on in life that I'm only human. So, I can admit that, at times, I've dropped the ball as well. But my beautiful children … they've taught me so much individually as well as collectively. I am so thankful for them. I do try to hide when I feel like I lack as a mother in certain circumstances or when I feel like I have faltered. I do that so they do not get to know about matters that do not concern children, just so that they would not have to worry about things that they don't need to worry about.

I believe a child should go and play and learn and enjoy life as children do, but my children are smart and intelligent, so nothing gets past them.

I can wholeheartedly admit that being a mother is the best experience that I've ever had. I absolutely love it. They always keep me on my toes for sure, and most of all, I love the memories we create together, and now that its just us, only me and my children, it has gotten even better. The memories that we create hold a value like no other. Because they're in their teens and preteens, I'm also able to allow the inner child in me to come out and play with them. They're incredibly funny for the most part. We're always laughing. Their personalities are so different, but their silliness is similar.

I love watching them get along and enjoy the little things in life. They sing together, dance, make tik-toks and even have play fights. We love each other and have each other's backs. They may fuss and fight at times, but they do not go against one another and I absolutely love this unity about them. They have taught me that being a mom is one of the greatest blessings in life. It does come with its pros and cons, to be honest. It comes with its ups and downs. But it is completely and entirely worth it. We love to be together, get angry at each other and have fun as well. We even cry together. It is a feeling of a family. Doing everything together and I absolutely love it. Another thing that I have absolutely adored is the ultimate strength that I've gained from being their mother. The blessings they bring and have brought to my life are far from none. There are not enough words, or things I can do or express to show how much gratitude I have for having them. I don't think even they understand what they mean to me. There were a few points in my life when I didn't feel like myself and feel worthy enough. As a mom, I didn't feel like I was giving them enough, spending enough time with them, loving them enough. I truly feel like I wasn't at times, but then, they were the ones who saved my life. They give me a reason to stay strong and to keep getting better, to fall down and to get back up, to pick myself back up on my own and keep pushing. To make something of myself and to show my children that what I always tell them I mean it and that's that. Giving up was now not even a thought.

I want my babies to know that anything that they want to achieve in life or would want to do or whoever they want to be. It is all possible. If they can dream it, they can achieve it. I want my babies to know that I'm their mother. I try my best to keep my children on the straight and narrow road. I need them only to know that whatever it is that they want to do, they have their mother's complete support! I do my best to teach my children the things in life and the ways from the lessons I've learned in life. All the wisdom and the experience that I get, I am passing it on to them. The right, the wrong. As a person, I don't know everything, but what I do know, I will always share it with them and continue to do so.

I have always kept a very open and communicative environment in my household with my children, and I've always made sure that they know that they can communicate and talk to me about anything. I've always raised them, making sure they know and understand this. They can tell me anything that is on their mind. I don't care what it is or how it would make me feel as their mother. Always want to and will always help them in their life no matter what. I will not be able to help them if I do not know what they're going through. As a mother, I will never judge them. I don't think it is my place. I just want them to learn. To experience, to love, be successful, and, ultimately, be the best they can be.

My Second Born

Two years after I was blessed with my firstborn, I found out that I was pregnant again. It was surprising for me, to be honest, to learn of this because a few days prior, I thought I got my period, which I later found out was implantation bleeding. I remember that during this faithful time, my then-boyfriend remained sick and was always throwing up. During the day, but even throughout the night as well. One day, out of the blue in the morning, he came to me and asked if I was pregnant. I told him that I wasn't. Even then, he decided to walk to the store and buy a box of pregnancy tests for me anyway.

Even though I was against taking the test initially, I decided to take it due to his persistence and to my surprise. Positive. He was so elated and ecstatic, but I remained, uh, confused about it. I could have sworn that I had had my period, so a few hours later, just to make sure, I took another test. The results of this test left no question or skepticism in me that I was pregnant because it came out positive again. So I accepted it and made my doctor's appointment.

Few weeks later, we finally heard the heartbeat. My boyfriend at the time shed a few tears of joy, true tears. I never asked him why he cried. I always assume that it was the excitement, that the reality is we were finally having a child together. Something we planned out when I was as young as 14 years old.

A few months passed by in an hour, and it was time for my ultrasound to make sure my baby was healthy and was about to come out. Also, I wanted to know what the gender of my baby was. During the ultrasound, I realized that God had not stopped his blessings on me because I got to know that I was going to have a boy. I was going to get what I always wanted. I was so excited about this. I was extremely anxious and nervous, but at the same time I was so optimistic about everything, about life, about myself, about my son who was going to come into the world. But what was even better was that I had already had a daughter, so now I have one of each. And for me, that was a big deal. I was so excited that I wanted to go out and buy boy things. Boy clothes, boy toys, anything boy. I could not control my excitement, so I was going to tell my whole family and let them know because my son was the first boy in the family. My other siblings had had girls, and so did I, but the first son of my family was about to come, and he was going to be mine. I was extremely excited to let my adopted mom know about him because I wanted to make her proud, and I also wanted her to know that I was going to give her her first grandson. So my boyfriend and I took some time out and went to her workplace after my ultrasound with the pictures to show her the surprise and hoping that she would be excited for us as well. When we told her about this awesome news, she was definitely shocked and surprised, but also excited and went out on her own to buy. His first set of Matchbox cars collection before he was even born. Later that day, she came to my house with all the new boy stuff. She had this part. It felt so amazing.

During the last few weeks of my pregnancy, I was getting a lot of Braxton Hicks (Contractions). So I was going in and out of the hospital, but mostly with false alarms. But soon enough, the day came when I was going into true labor. I didn't believe it even then, but I went to the hospital anyway. I was told that it was another false alarm for me and that I should go home and take a hot bath. So I took their advice and did exactly what they told me. But while I was in my bath, my contractions had stopped, so I thought that all of a sudden, they would come back with a vengeance. So, little surprise here: back to the hospital we went to, and after hours and hours of contractions, it was time for me to push. It was so surprising for me because it was really easy for me to push him out. I do not do much, actually. He did all the work on his own. Yeah, this boy pushed himself out.

When he came out after hours, I remember seeing that my son was bubbling from his mouth. It scared me so much that it rattled me, so I called on my nurse to come in quickly. She came running in to see what was going on. And calm my nerves. After checking him out, she let me know that he was perfectly fine, and that he was just drooling.

Having him was such an experience. To be honest. For example, he is the first boy for me. I initially had no idea and no clue how to even change him. Of course, I knew how to change diapers and everything, but changing him felt quite different. His dad showed me and. That is how I learned how to do it. Also, as he got older, he started showing how much energy he had, which was a different experience than what I had previously experienced.

I started paying an awful lot of attention to his energy levels, but I also eventually realized that he wasn't talking as much as I felt he should for a boy his age. During one of his doctor's appointments, I brought up this concern. And the doctor referred me to early intervention for his speech delay. So, during his early intervention sessions, they taught us both— my son and I—sign language. They also taught me to use sign language while saying the words by pointing at my mouth and asking him to pay close attention so that he could understand what I was saying, and could eventually repeat it himself as well.

Years down the road, I became more and more concerned about his energy levels. His hyperactivity and impulsivity were a concern for me. By comparing him to my oldest, I started to feel like something was terribly wrong. I took him to the hospital again because I was getting extremely anxious due to certain things that he had been doing that just didn't seem right to me. He was eventually diagnosed with ADHD. It made me realize that my concerns as a mother for my child stand true. But then again, I had no idea what ADHD even was.

On my own, I decided to do some research and educate myself about what my child was going through. My dear boy. So I went to the store one afternoon to buy a notebook, pens, and highlighters and I decided to go on YouTube to watch and learn through videos and make as many notes as possible. I was determined to teach and educate myself, so I knew how to better help him and myself.

When he started kindergarten, I had his school put on a referral to get him on IEP because his teacher had seen that he was delayed. So, I did some more research and found out through his eye doctor that he was having trouble learning about colors because he was colorblind.

After finally getting him on an IEP, fighting tooth and nail, I knew and felt like he wasn't getting treated correctly there. But more importantly, he did not get the service that I believe he deserved or needed.

It was when he switched schools that he began to actually flourish. He still had a delay in reading, but I could see that he was improving tremendously. While he was there, they all had also put him in a smaller classroom. *Finally*, I thought. Unfortunately, as he got into a higher grade, he had to switch schools again because they didn't have a smaller class for the grade he was going into. During summer school, at a new school, he was later diagnosed with dyslexia, which made so much sense as to why he was struggling with his reading.

When he entered his first grade, I decided to put him in football. He originally began with flag football until he got into his third grade. That's when he actually started playing contact football. And has been playing ever since. I absolutely love it because it has been his outlet for getting a lot of his hyperactivity out. May I also mention how amazingly talented this boy is. He is extremely good at football. I so love watching him play, and I've definitely been the loudest mom in the stands throughout all his games. During his freshman year of high school, he became the back backup quarterback for junior varsity and also played as a wide receiver. I was so proud of my son.

I would like to take this moment to just say something. One of the things that I have learned being a boy mom is that they may not be good from a societal standpoint, in some areas of their life, but God always makes up for it in other places for him. For my son, football, or any other sport for that matter, is where my son excelled. I see so much beauty in it that I am overwhelmed to learn of his talents. He can also draw amazingly and can build just about anything.

My son has taught me so much that is precious to me in life and is also important. For one, patience. He has also taught me that love is a matter that is quite different when it comes to having a son. My two girls always tell me that my son is my favorite, and in all honesty, he kind of is. I'm just kidding. To be honest, the bond between a mother and her son, especially her first son, is completely different and unexplainable.

He also taught me that even if we have our disabilities, we must also be our own advocates and must learn and teach our own selves so that nobody can change us or tell us how to go about our lives when it comes to education. And that is what I want, for him to get all the services and the amenities he needs and deserves.

He also taught me to fight and take my stand for what I believe to be right and true and to never give up.

He's taught me the truth behind being a boy mom. Going to his practices and traveling with him to his away games and, most certainly, his home games, throwing the ball around with him, experiencing him, growing into a young man, listening to him yell and scream, playing Fortnite with my nephew and his friends.

I am so grateful and appreciative of the fact that he always checks up on me to see if I am doing alright and that I am okay and give me random hugs and kisses on my cheeks. He never leaves the house without saying, "Mommy, I love you." And doesn't let me reply, "I love you, too," and says, "Nope. You say, 'I love you more.' And doesn't leave until I say it.

Christine Pimental

My Third Born

Soon after, living my life with my youngest son and my eldest, a month after my birthday, I found out that I was pregnant again with my youngest. I was over the moon because we were planning for another pregnancy.

The pregnancy went somewhat great, except for my extreme sickness to strike me again, as it did with my oldest. And towards the end, I had become extremely uncomfortable. She had gone head down at about the six-month span of my pregnancy, so it became quite painful to walk, sit, lay down, stand or even bathe.

I, along with everyone else, was so excited to find out that we were going to be blessed with a baby girl once more, especially him because she was going to be his first biological daughter. I was so happy that we were going to be blessed with her.

We had already picked out a name for her because I was going to name my son this name had he been a girl, but I had been blessed with a boy. With her, I instinctually knew that I was going to have a girl, just by how sick I had remained throughout. With my son, I had only nausea. But with my oldest, I could not stop throwing up, and this pregnancy felt the same.

A few months later, I went into labor, similar to how I had gone into labor with my son. I was having what I thought were false contractions, so I took a hot bath for myself. They stopped momentarily, but all of a sudden, as I was getting out, they came back with a vengeance.

My youngest was the first labor I didn't have to use Pitocin. She had labored well with my body, and my body had labored all on its own, which was.

When it was time for me to push, I felt like I had dilated super flash. My water never broke, so when it was time to push her out, she came out still in her amniotic SAC. It was so amazing to see and witness. I was in complete amazement because they had the mirror right in front of me. So I got to watch the whole thing, and even after she was delivered, they let her stay in the bag on the table for a few minutes as we just watched her in amazement because none of us, not even the nurses, had ever seen this experience before.

As she got older, she loved to play pretend. She loved to play with dolls and fake food and loved to dress up as well. Her favorite show was "Doc Mcstuffin". She would also play with all of her Doc Mcstuffin toys and would even stay in her dressed-up clothes all day. She was extremely adorable and is to this day as well.

As she got older, because she had always been a hyperactive person herself, I put her in cheerleading for a while, and while she was in school, she played basketball as well, which was something that she always enjoyed, and it showed on her face as well.

Christine Pimental

As she got older and through my noticing and observation of her, I realized that my youngest is an empathic human. She is extremely nurturing, caring, loving, but also a very humorous and goofy girl. To my surprise, she also behaves like a mother to her elder brother. I tell them all the time. They're like two peas in a pod, and when they get older, I can see them living with each other because although they're siblings, like everyone else, they do have their moments when they feel down and unenergetic, they joke and uplift each other and come through for each other. For me, it just goes to show how close they are, taking care of each other in times of distress, and I absolutely love it.

She's also very close to her elder sister. They act silly together. They're always laughing, joking, ordering out and sitting in their room, sneaking food together. They also love to make lots of different tik-toks together. They love to sing and dance with one another and laugh about it as well. I love that they have such cherishable moments. Even though her sister is a few years older than her, I love how they spend time and hang out with one another and can relate to each other on most things.

I feel like my youngest taught me to be a more nurturing person than I had believed I was. She also taught me to be more affectionate and more present. She absolutely loves to talk, so she will leave me no choice but to give her my full attention because she's very sensitive. So if you're not looking at her while she talks, she feels like you're not listening or that you don't care, and because I knew how it felt to not feel heard. At times, I try to always be present with her in the moment, and if I couldn't, I vocalized to let her know that as her mom who loves her, I see her and hear her, but, in some moments, I am busy as well. So I would ask her to give me a minute so that I could finish whatever I was doing and give her my full and undivided attention. Truth be told, I love that we are so transparent and open in our communication with each other. It is quite helpful that we are all very understanding of each other.

She also taught me how to be open to being a kid at heart again. This past Christmas, she bought me a pink teddy bear with a Disney Princess coloring book and some colored pencils as well. Little did she know, which I eventually told her about, as a child, coloring was my favorite thing to do. It was always something I would be doing, along with relaxing, listening to music and doing puzzles. So, I was extremely thankful for her gifts because, again, it allowed me to be a kid at heart again. We even spent a few hours, me, her and my oldest, sitting on my bed one day, listening to music and coloring while my son was playing one of his games.

Chapter Nine

Spiritual Awakening

After the unexpected passing of my sister, the series of events that followed threw me completely off emotionally. I had a miscarriage with a pregnancy, like with my other three children, I desperately wanted. I didn't think I could get pregnant anymore after having my youngest, so I decided to go through some painful testing prior to the miscarriage, only to find ot there's nothing wrong. So when I finally got pregnant again, especially after just experiencing a major loss, I was devastated. The deep depression I was already experiencing sent me even deeper. "To help" with my state of mind after losing my sister, I started smoking weed to help with sleep. After the miscarriage, I began to smoke even more, all day... every day.

After I stopped talking and interacting with my "siblings" partially because I felt like when I lost my sister, they weren't there for me emotionally. Honestly, I feel like NO ONE was except for one of my old "friends". I made it a point to stay high all day. I never wanted to be sober.

I also began to sleep a lot more, due to just trying to escape my reality.

How I had seen my reality at the time was all with my real, actual biological family, who are now gone... I'm alone. I'm no longer speaking to so-called friends and family because I felt as if no one cared about how and what I was feeling and how I was trying to cope with my trial for a relationship with my children's father was looking like it was next to go.

I remember before the breakup, we were sitting in the back of my home smoking and we were discussing me no longer dealing with my family and friends. I remember telling him that I feel like there're more things in life that need to go, and I hope it ain't him. I said that because although I had already got rid of a lot that I felt wasn't serving me in the right way, I still didn't feel like I was complete in a way. Well, a few months later, the breakup did indeed happen. Fifteen years down the drain, well at least that's how it felt, and all hell broke loose inside myself. Immediately after the breakup, I was so broken that I went on medical leave from work and started counseling, like literally the someday of the split because I honestly felt like if I didn't, I wasn't gonna make it.

I would always talk to his biological dad before his unexpected passing, and he would, in the moment, help me through my emotions. I remember he would repeatedly remind me that I have to stay strong and pick myself up because my children need me. He would also tell me that it's ok to feel hurt and betrayed but I can't stay there. I have to get up! One of the most important things he said to me was that I was getting back up, picking myself up, and I needed to fully armor myself. If I'm being honest, I had NO CLUE what he meant by that until now. But I must say, I thank him for being a listening ear, a shoulder to cry on, but also an angel in the physical who helped and guided me emotionally to regain my strength to better myself. Butt also knew that this was going to be one of the biggest fights of my life. Not a physical fight but an emotional, mental, and spiritual fight. He wasn't lying. I'm extremely grateful and thankful for all the great love and advice he gave me because although some of it made sense, some of it didn't, but it's definitely begun.

One night, after a day of crying, smoking, and just being frustrated, I sat in my backhall, high out of my mind, just screaming, yelling to GOD because I didn't understand why all of this was happening; why did he take my family; why did he take my relationship; why did he make me get rid of all that I knew? My mom's biological sister called me, and during our conversation, it felt like my mom was speaking to me through her. One of the questions she asked me was, "Why are you so mad?" I just remember her saying, "Christine, why are you so angry? You've been like this you're whole life and everyone can see it."

Without hesitation, I replied back, "I'm angry because everybody leaves me and it started with my mom and dad.

They gave me up. Why have me if you didn't want me?" At this point, I was crying to her in complete shambles, but for whatever reason, I felt like it was my mom speaking to me, asking me this.

My aunt said, "They didn't give you up, Christine; you guys were taken from them. They loved you guys; they just couldn't get it together. They tried."

Honestly, when I processed that, it felt a little better knowing that they didn't abandon us. They were just too sick to get themselves together to be the best parents to me, my sister, and my brother that they could be.

My whole life, I was told that she (my mom) had given us up. So, it instilled immense anger in me. And then, as I got older and people came in and out of my life, it validated to me that I wasn't worthy, at that time, anyway.

With that information from my aunt my mom's biological sister) I decided and realized she was right. Maybe all of this is happening in my life because it's time for me to heal. To finally sit down and really take a real good hard look within and start to heal myself out of all the trauma I've been through. Like really and truly face everything I've been through in the past and heal it so I can be more at peace and better myself not only for me but as a role model for my children and my sister's children. It was time, I must say. The healing process of me facing my past didn't start right away. For that, I gave myself one month to stay on leave from work to cry, smoke, be angry and depressed, and allow myself to just grieve the loss of what I had gone through; all the hurt and pain was forever my prison.

After that month, I went back to physically working but also mentally and emotionally. I began to pray more than I ever had in my entire life, asking God so many questions but also asking him for guidance. During one of my breakdowns, I remember crying on the floor in my bathroom (thinking I was hiding it from my children, and becoming extremely suicidal. My oldest walked in and sat beside me and asked me if I was okay while holding me in her arms. I explained and cried, telling her that I was tired. My soul was tired. I was mentally and emotionally tired. I didn't want to live anymore. I said, "My mom, dad, brother, and sister were gone. Maybe I need to join them; I don't want to be here alone."

She grabbed my face and said, "Mommy, you can't leave us; you're all we have. We need you, and so do my cousins. Aunty's not here anymore, so all we have is you." I just remember repeatedly crying, saying, "I can't, I just can't," while shaking my head no. Something in me wouldn't allow me to give up on myself besides the thought that my daughter was, in fact, a hundred percent right at this point. I'm all these babies have. Little did she know that that night, it wasn't her who needed me; it was I who needed her, and she came through… she saved me… from me.

After that, I decided to quit smoking weed and sober up. Not realizing I was actually breaking a general curse of substance abuse by doing so. In doing this, I started to ask more questions, just trying to find out what was going on with me. I eventually started to do research through Google and YouTube, but more so through giving time to myself and fighting my own demons by doing some inner work on my soul and my spirit. I feel like God had led me to what it was. I was going through a "spiritual awakening" and, at that point, an actual ego death. At that time, my ego had to die so I could be reborn into a better me.

While more and more going to counseling, I began journaling more and more. I decided that instead of doing what I used to do, and that was jumping from relation: ship to relationship, I could no longer run from myself. It was time to face my biggest opponent… ME! It wasn't easy. It's never easy facing yourself, especially when you've spent your whole life running and numbing. Distracting even. Well, that wasn't an option anymore. In order for me to find myself and figure out why I was going through everything I was going through, I had to start to unpack all my experiences, especially the traumatic ones, starting from day one of my life up until now because, of course, I'm still healing. Accepting that we'll never be fully healed, we can definitely clean up from within instead of looking outward and placing blame on everyone around us. Realizing and accepting the fact that, at some point, we aid and play a part in our experiences.

Holding myself accountable for the part I played in a lot of my relationships, both romantic and platonic, was hard. Literally asking myself what part I played was very eye-opening for me.

I realized that I was extremely broken due to my childhood of not feeling worthy, feeling different, not heard, not seen, emotionally and physically. I, in turn, attracted as I got older relationships and friendships that mirrored back to me all those feelings. So, I began to lower my worth and please people. Just to keep people around because my biggest fear was being alone. But on the contrary, no matter who was around, I felt alone anyway,

It's funny how, prior to the breakup, I was at work, and one of my kids called me to let me know their dad was drunk. Stumbling around and yelling at them. Something I got used to because he drank all day every day. I met him this way and just accepted it but this day was different. I was fed up, so while driving home, I prayed to God and asked Him to change my life. Whatever and whoever got to go, do what He has to do. I'll follow His plan for me. I say all that to say, even though I didn't see change right away, as I look at my life now and look back at all I've been through, and everyone He's removed from my life. It's like He was just waiting for me to call on Him.

During that time in my life, I remember feeling like I didn't know who I was anymore. Looking in the mirror not recognizing who I saw. I knew it was time for a change; what I didn't know was that it'd be this extensive and, at times, dramatic. But it's definitely been worth it. While going through this journey, I've learned so much. I've learned, first of all, to ALWAYS listen to your intuition. I didn't; I used to think it was just anxiety. Now I rely on it heavily. I also learned that it is actually very peaceful being alone. I didn't like it at first when God forced me into isolation to find myself, but it's not that bad. I actually do it on my own at times to recharge myself and gain inner clarity. To ground myself and balance my emotions when I feel off. I've learned that all the love I was trying to give others, I need to be giving to myself. Self-love should always be top priority.

I've also learned that I am worthy and deserving of love no matter what I've been through in my past. I've learned that when people show me a negative side of themselves, I need to believe them the first time. Believe the red flags you see when they show them. Learn to be selfish (in a positive way) for yourself. Put yourself first and it's okay to tell people no. Especially when you truly don't want to do something. You've got to put yourself first because if I'm not right within, I can't be right for others. This healing journey has taught me what I do and don't want in my life and what I will and will no longer accept in my life. How I want to be treated, how I want to be loved. It's taught me to be very protective of myself now. I feel like the whole point of this was for me to learn the lessons. From how I was allowing others to treat me and what I allowed and accepted just to keep them around me.

One of my biggest lessons was to pray. Pray no matter what, good and bad. I used to go through so much shit, and instead of praying, I'd just sit in this victim mentality of why me instead of praying and surrendering it to GOD. But now, I look for the lesson in it so I can heal it, accept it, and move forward with what NOT to do or allow ever again. It's crazy because I used to look back at my life and feel like I wasn't progressing because I didn't see a change on the "outside", but what I've realized is I've actually made so much progress on the inside with my healing and newfound knowledge and wisdom. That it's only a matter of time, it reflects on the outside.

It's so much more important to heal the inner you because when you're at peace and content with yourself, it's bound to show on the outside.

Again, self-love and respect for myself are what's most important to me right now. As sad as it sounds, it's something I never gave myself in the past. I feel like it was because I was (in the past) so used to putting people, places, and things above myself due to, as a child, not feeling important, seen, enough, or worthy. So again, as an adult, that was all I attracted to myself. But now, through healing, I acknowledge that and know that's not true. In fact, it's the complete opposite. I feel and know that I am very worthy, deserving, important, seen, creative, beautiful (inside and out), divinely protected, calm, at peace, knowledgeable, smart, talented, and unstoppable. I thank God because before this, my awakening and rebirth, I didn't know these things about myself. Oh, and let's not forget how "independent" and spiritually guided and protected I am.

I've also learned that it is a MUST to have boundaries and standards. Never accept less than what I give myself and how I treat myself. Let go, release, and accept the past and move forward UNAPOLOGETICALLY! Put your blinders on and never look back. There's no reason to, nor is it helpful to dwell on it. I thank everyone from my past, though, in all honesty. I've learned and am still learning not to allow anyone or anything from the past back into my new life, at least not like they were before. I'm too important and way too loving to go back to what hurt me; one of my goals in life is to help people, even if it's just one. To be able to help and guide them through situations similar to mine. To remind them that they MATTER! For me, to now use what I've been through to help others is truly a lesson and gift in itself. And makes all of it worth it. Just to have come out on the other side is a blessing. Although I'm still Learning, healing, and creating a new life for myself, my children, and my sister's children (my other babies), I REFUSE to give up. There's more for me to do and more to be written, so. LET'S GOOO!!!

Chapter Ten

LOVE… What I "thought" It was vs. What It Now means to Me

I used to believe "being in love" meant staying around situations for friendships, relationships, and family through the ups and downs, good or bad, and no matter if it becomes toxic, deteriorative, corrosive, venomous or unhealthy to do so. I also thought it meant staying through "thick and thin". That's loyalty, which you deal with when you "LOVE" someone. Accepting disrespect, unfaithfulness, betrayal, lies, belittlement, hurt, put-downs, disloyalty, people pleasing, draining your energy at the expense of others, constantly giving and barely, if ever, being reciprocated back to, never saying "No", always being the go-to person for people to let out their angst within because I can take it and I will because I love them, and constantly doing so by being an ear that listens… someone whom people could look up to for any kind of help. Let me just say… yes, you should be like that, love like that, but sometimes, not everyone deserves your true heart unless they earn it, especially when it's never reciprocated. Love now is being patient with myself and teaching ourselves how to be emotionally balanced. Accepting that I'm going to have days where I feel super happy and excited for life, being optimistic about whatever is to come. But, at the same time, to always know that I will also have to accept my days or moments where I question or worry and remain anxious about what's to come because I've never been there. The dangling dance on the thin rope of uncertainty is always a daunting venture. I still grieve my past and the experiences, but I also pray through it and keep on reminding myself that even though I felt every emotion and cultivated every feeling within my mind, body and soul, I lived through it; it was not able to ruin me in terms of emotionality. In fact, it helped me make sense of a lot of questions about my life. By sitting with myself and feeling all that was going on inside me, I finally found that it was okay… and I was okay. I'm safe; my mind and my emotions are safe.

Love is putting yourself first. Allowing yourself to rest when needed. No, you're not lazy! As a mother… a single mother, I have a lot on my plate mostly, and trying to heal myself mentally and emotionally, on top of working, cooking and cleaning, waking my children up in the morning for school, taking them to their appointments, be on call in case they need me for things when they're away from me, or I'm away from them, making sure I'm present for them so I can enjoy every moment with them but also make sure they're constantly pushing for better and doing what they need to do. It's a lot on one person.

So, when my body is tired, I'm learning to allow myself to rest and not feel guilty for it.

Love is no longer tolerating what you KNOW you do not deserve. If people aren't treating you the way you treat yourself, then you need to leave them behind. And always remember people treat you how they truly feel about themselves. It has nothing to do with you and ALL to do with them, especially when you're truly loving yourself, respecting yourself, nurturing yourself, and being kind to yourself.

Love my own self for me is spending time with friends, going out, trying new things, coming out of my comfort zone, traveling, laughing and joking and goofing around, surrounded by people I love and who love me, or just hanging out or being on the phone enjoying each other's conversation and time.

Love is spending time with my children, nephew, and nieces, laughing, joking, hanging out, watching movies, watching them be silly, just watching them grow. Always showing them and reminding them how much I love them.

Love is also spending time alone, healing, journaling, listening to music, singing, and dancing… ALONE, engaging in activities that make me feel good, like getting my nails done, doing my hair, coloring, watching my favorite TV shows, and sometimes taking myself out to eat, going to the car wash, or even walking to the store. I'm so proud of myself for doing a lot more things alone because prior to my healing journey, I used to remain frightened at just the thought of being alone, let alone doing things by myself. That is a major change for me, as previously I was entirely uncomfortable to even speak the words… Alone. But now, I'm used to it and have begun to enjoy it. It is addictive, to be honest.

Love to me is peace. A total peace, mentally and emotionally, even environmentally at times. Personally, I have grown up and also been in relationships and friendships where I was surrounded by a lot of people and a lot of noise, attending parties and music so loud that my mind would go numb with my body. Now, I love and appreciate just sitting in pure solitude, being able to hear my own thoughts, and just allowing my mind to be completely quiet… a tranquility of sorts. My children… relaxing, doing their own thing, while I'm relaxing… and doing my own thing.

Love is knowing my worth, knowing what I deserve and fighting for it, setting standards and setting boundaries, but most importantly, standing firm on them. So if that means distancing myself from people, places, and things that mean me no well, nor do they serve a positive purpose in my life… oh well. Here, I must put myself first and love and show myself what I deserve… actually giving myself all the love I kept trying to so badly give everyone else.

Love for self is setting goals and actually achieving them, and focusing on what's important to me. My wants, my needs, my legacy, not only that but also being a positive role model to all the kids (mine and my sisters), showing them that no matter what you're going through in life, you never give up on yourself. And ANYTHING YOU set your mind on, you can, with hard work, focus, dedication, and consistency you can achieve it.

I've always told myself this phrase, and I've continued and will continue to live by it. "Never allow pain to conquer you. Always turn your pain into POWER!" If I can pass anything on to the kids is just … "Winning is the ONLY option!"

I must say, I'm so thankful to GOD for helping me get back on my feet and to keep on being grounded and remembering "Who I Am!" I'm grateful that I'm on a spiritual journey, a healing journey, because I look at life, and now myself as well, so differently. I can wholeheartedly say I love myself now, I appreciate myself, and I see and actually love all my qualities, good and bad, because, let's be real here, none of us are perfect. I actually hug and kiss myself sometimes… (*silly, I know*), but that's truly how much I care about myself. I actually look at myself in the mirror and LOVE who and what I see.

Love to me is literally loving the skin I am in, loving the fact that I am different, and it is okay that I am misunderstood at times. At the end of the day, I realized that I'm a sweetheart who always has the best for people at heart, but I can also be very fiery if need be. I speak up, I speak my mind, and I go on rants sometimes, but one of the lessons I've learned over the span of my life is to remain balanced, knowing that I have the control to pick and choose, to be emotionally composed. This is the same philosophy of ancient Japan talking about Yin-Yang, and so many others speak the same. To this day, I remain proud of what I have accomplished on my own, judging myself by how I used to be and reacted around people, places, and things because I had zero self-control in the past due to past trauma and to whom I have become.

"Darkness cannot drive out darkness, only light can do that. Hate cannot drive out hate, only love can do that."

~Dr. Martin Luther King Jr.

Acknowledgments

First and foremost, I want to thank everyone involved in helping me make this memoir happen. This is one of my most PROUDEST achievements in life and one I've worked extremely hard on. I want my whole team to know how much gratitude I have for them and thank them so much for being such a huge part of this journey with me; words can't even begin to express how I feel and how thankful I truly am.

The first two people I want to give thanks, appreciation, and recognition to are Ryan Hall (my team lead) and Frank Shaw (my senior project manager) for being here from the beginning of all of this. Showing me the ropes and never leaving my side. I want to give a very special thanks, appreciation, and recognition to you. Zane Cooper (my project manager) came on the team later in this journey and ignited a fire in me to keep going and not give up, which I never knew I had. I thank him so much and give him the utmost gratitude for always calling and checking up on me in life in general, even besides my book. He's just such an amazing and caring person. I'm so glad he's apart of this book and my life altogether. Last but not least, I want to thank Jazz Jeffery (my senior content specialist) for helping with the creation and edits of all of this.

About the Author

Christine Marie, youngest of three, single mother and biological aunt of three. She is the first in her family to graduate high school and also graduated with her cosmetology license. She is confidant, smart, caring, loving, and nurturing. Her life has been full of ups and downs from the start, but she's healing and evolving from her past trauma and childhood traumas on a consistent basis so she can now remain peaceful and healthy mentally, emotionally, physically, and spiritually.

Christine is learning throughout her healing journey that not every day is going to be sunshine and rainbows however, you have to go through to get through. Tomorrow's gonna be a better day. Her motto in life now is, "Winning is the ONLY option; giving up is NOT!"

www.ingramcontent.com/pod-product-compliance
Lightning Source LLC
Chambersburg PA
CBHW040241130526
44590CB00049B/4122